Solo

For my sons Bradley and Joel. 'May you both find your own freedoms in life.'

Solo

A thousand miles from anywhere

Dave Clarke

BLUE DOLPHIN
BOOKS

Copyright © Dave Clarke 2012
First published in 2012 by Blue Dolphin Books,
www.amolibros.co.uk

Distributed by Gardners Books, 1 Whittle Drive, Eastbourne,
East Sussex, BN23 6QH
Tel: +44 (0) 1323 521555 | Fax: +44 (0) 1323 521666

British Library Cataloguing in Publication Data.
A catalogue record for this book is available from the British
Library.

ISBN 978-0-9555124-1-4

Typeset by Amolibros, Milverton, Somerset
www.amolibros.com
This book production has been managed by Amolibros
Printed and bound by T J International Ltd, Padstow, Cornwall, UK

'Out here the weather becomes your friend and your enemy. The sea will tease you with her rhythmic playfulness or worry you into prayer and forgiveness, repenting past sins in the hope of freedom from the tempest. But she will forever be tempting you back…'

Dave Clarke, 2012

Contents

List of Illustrations

Facing page 46

Acknowledgements

IT IS WITHOUT DOUBT that I have many, many people to thank for making the whole project and eventual journey to row solo across the Atlantic a success. These people have enriched me throughout my quest to complete what was for me an adventure of a lifetime.

For me it is not merely the journey but the people you meet when travelling it. The following named people I owe special thanks, as without their help and support the project would never have been a success.

The real journey began when first meeting Kenneth Crutchlow from the Ocean Rowing Society at London's Boat Show in early 2007. Ken's enthusiasm for the sport of ocean rowing had me hooked. His knowledge and generosity in sharing it really helped form an early plan of where to start. Also around in those early days was Simon Chalk of Woodvale Challenge Ltd, a source of invaluable information in getting a plan together. He always had time to share his thoughts and opinions.

And of course the dream team that designed and built Solo. Phil Morrison for a superbly designed new class of solo ocean rowing boat. Not only is Phil a top naval architect but also a great host who made sure there was always a welcoming meal and room whenever I visited his home.

Jamie and Emily of Global Boat Works for crafting what I can only describe as a piece of art. Nothing was too much trouble and I was proud to own a boat built by Jamie. It was a privilege to witness the skill and effort of Global Boat Works while building Solo.

Peter Litton for the electrics and making sure there would be no electrical malfunctions on the journey.

For all my family, especially the understanding and patience of my wife Elaine and my sons Bradley and Joel.

To all my friends, the old ones who have always been there for me and the new ones I've met doing this project. Special thanks to Phil Lancashire for always being there to lend a hand and buy me beer. For all the sponsors and companies that helped me out with funds, equipment and generous discounts. All the people who donated money to SportsAid and the East Cheshire Hospice, my chosen charities.

And a final word to John Holloway who has encouraged my writing over many years. His guidance, talent and friendship have kept me focused throughout. Thank you.

Foreword

FAMOUS ADVENTURERS ARE NO more heroic or brave than men and women less known. Celebrity has no place with those who seize the opportunity to realise their dreams, no matter their calling or station in life. They hear the echo of Goethe... 'Whatever you can do or dream to do, begin it.'

In this book you will meet an ordinary man with a deeply embedded passion for adventure and discovery; not just of the natural world but of himself. A man who seeks not fame or fortune but the stirring of his soul that led him to challenge fear, pain, uncertainty but also to experience joy, confidence and an indefinable sense of personal freedom.

Having already sailed thousands of miles alone and unaided across the Atlantic Ocean, Dave Clarke set out to row the same journey, again solo, having never rowed in his life. A year in the planning, his incredible journey involved physical and emotional turbulence for himself and his family. His story cannot fail to impress; an ordinary man doing extraordinary things.

The world needs adventurers – Dave Clarke is surely one of them: you might be too.

Ranulph Fiennes

Introduction

IN 1993 I SAILED over 5,000 miles, solo and unaided across the vast emptiness that is the north Atlantic Ocean. I was twenty-eight years old. My boat Sharky, at six-and-a-bit metres long was one of the smallest yachts ever to have made the journey. The whole project took more than three years after leaving Falmouth, with numerous high and low points along the way, and moments of sheer delight and utter terror. I wanted to capture the experiences for my old age and as a legacy for others, perhaps to inspire them to reach for their own challenges in life; perhaps to prove that there are no barriers to ambition.

I'd been around boats for much of my life and enjoyed the mysterious and often unfathomable grip that the sea has on people; primeval, elemental, enduring. Water's edge or on the deep are places from which to dream, to question, to wonder about life and self: a timeless seascape of restless waves; an amphitheatre of potential energy and personal aspiration.

I chose to sail the Atlantic, not because I wanted to but because I needed to: an inexplicable calling to experience one of the great environments where freedom of mind, body and spirit is as infinite as the inaccessible horizons. The sea's restlessness matched that of my own life; wanting something more but not knowing what. Sailing coastal waters fed and partially satiated that desire but on one exhilarating voyage across the Channel the gathering thoughts of many years finally coalesced; I challenged myself to sail one of the great oceans. Completing that challenge taught me much about myself, about my limitations and my capabilities. Returning home fulfilled, I swore I would never undertake such a journey again: my restlessness had been sublimated.

But the sea cannot be so easily dismissed. I returned to a busy life, to a new business challenge and marriage. I threw myself into fresh opportunities and responsibilities, invigorated by my solo achievements, confident I had my future mapped out.

But I'd not reckoned with distant memories lapping at the shores of my mind. In quiet moments of reflection I returned to my experiences, time enhancing the high points and conveniently diminishing the pain and tribulations. I found solace in the reminiscence of a calm azure ocean, the exhilaration of sunsets that were exclusively mine – and the ultimate prize – alone with my own freedoms, beholden to no one, at peace with myself and my environment. The constant gales and squalls, the misery of a damp, stinking cabin, the times I thought I would drown, were never forgotten, but I could glory in their defeat. I had survived them, had I not?

A dozen or so years later and fully immersed in my male midlife crisis, the restlessness returned. Now with a young family and owning a successful business, my life had perhaps become a tad too comfortable. I still climbed mountains, walked the Peak District hills and went off-road on my bike, but these were transitory delights; single days away from work to reconnect with nature. My thoughts kept returning to the possibility of another big project. I'd heard someone mention that you're only as good as your next challenge and it stuck like glue. Was it just a trite phrase or a gauntlet thrown down at my feet? The thought wormed and buried itself in my being. Could I? Should I? Would I?

In 2007 I heard again the siren sound of those ceaseless waves. I decided to retrace my route across the Atlantic, but this time I would row, solo and again unsupported. The notion took hold and anchored itself. I spent a long time in the safe harbour of research but, as you'll discover in Chapter One, in an unguarded moment I was propelled into the tidal surge of reality. Fate had intervened. I was going to row the Atlantic. I'd somehow forgotten that I'd never been in a rowing boat of any description.

You might think that this venture was merely a repeat of past adventures, but nothing could be further from the truth. The old feelings remained: panic, fear, frustration, elation, wonderment, contentment, but the experiences were completely new. I had set myself an equally difficult and complex project, finding fresh hurdles and levels of self-doubt. Ultimately I rediscovered the greatest elixir of them all: freedom.

As with *An Ocean Away*, this book is not a technical manual or an attempt at self-glorification. It's a warts-and-all journey of extreme challenge that in one form or another is within us all. A personal testing that searches out weaknesses, discovers new strengths and forces us to live beyond our self-ordained comfort zone. Personal challenges are what make us who we are and who we become: unique individuals living our lives, forever changing, forever moving on, forever doubting, forever striving to improve. Forever hoping.

The sea is a great metaphor for life. When next you sit at its shore I hope you feel the synergy of restlessness that makes us human. I hope you experience a harmony with the constantly searching ebb and flow.

And I hope you find your own personal freedom.

Dave Clarke, 2012

CHAPTER ONE

A Stage is Set

'This is Dave,' he said. 'He's going to row the Atlantic...'

I COULDN'T REALLY TAKE my eyes off him. The scars on his face were deep, fanned out like the petals of a large summer daisy. Five of them about an inch long, etched on proud cheekbones. As he turned I caught a glimpse of his other cheek and saw the same figuration. The symmetry was remarkable: surgeon-like precision, though likely carried out by village elders as he reached puberty. I studied his features and guessed him to be about sixty; perhaps an elder himself, now carrying out the same ritualistic practices.

His skin was ebony black; a deep burnt black that not only comes from skin pigment but from years under a baking sun. Yellowed eyes still had fight in them, glistening with the flicker of youth trapped in an aging body; but they had a depth that drew me in and I momentarily felt guilty as I trespassed within his thoughts. I imagined arid landscapes where he would hunt game and defend his village; imagined the colourful costumes and ochre painted faces; his neck graced with stones and wood gathered from nature's never-ending store. I envied the simple lifestyle of the hunter gatherer, of modest, happy village life where survival takes precedence.

My mind was shaken from its reverie by the swerve and heavy

braking of the train. The doors hissed open. I'd been staring at the guy opposite since he'd boarded the tube several stations ago; wondering who he was, dressed in a suit, carrying a briefcase. He looked familiar but I was certain I didn't know him. Then a memory from years before snapped into focus. He reminded me of a street pedlar I'd spotted in the Cape Verde Islands some years ago during my solo sail across the Atlantic Ocean; one of those unforgettable faces that imprints on the mind. He left the carriage, looking straight through me with those mesmeric eyes as I dragged myself back to reality. What the hell was I doing on the Underground? My thoughts tuned in again to the present. It was early January 2007 and I'd been to meet Kenneth Cruchlow from the Ocean Rowing Society (ORS). We'd met at the London Boat Show where he'd introduced me to a few other people with him. 'This is Dave,' he said. 'He's going to row the Atlantic... .' This was a heck of a shock because I'd been entertaining the idea for only about three weeks or so. A general information enquiry to ORS before Christmas had resulted in an invitation to meet Ken at the London Boat Show. Now all of a sudden I'd been presented as an ocean-going rower! The egotistical wimp in me refused to admit it was just an idea with which I'd been flirting; the impulsive idiot bit just nodded and smiled while the tiny level-headed part of my brain screamed, 'What the devil have you just done?!!' This was a defining moment. Now I had a real and serious project on my hands. Apparently I'd committed myself: I really *was* going to row the Atlantic, an idea that I'd mentally diarised for January 2008. Gulp. Now I had an even bigger challenge: how to convince my wife Elaine. An ocean row was going to be a piece of cake by comparison!

The meeting with Ken was unusual; a character so full of life and enthusiasm, matched by his eccentric, mad professor looks, shoulder-length hair and a whiskery moustache that would make a walrus envious. He was accompanied by Virginia, a French lady working for ARGOS, a French company that distributed satellite beacons to would-be ocean rowers. Also present was Victor, Ken's Russian brother-in-law, also harbouring thoughts of rowing an ocean. The final guy at the table was Matt Boreham, who'd been in the first ocean rowing race back in 1997, organised by Chay Blyth. Matt had abandoned his attempt thirty days in, also having to scupper an attempted row from Canada to England some years later. He'd finally made a successful solo row from the Canaries to Antigua on his third attempt, so he was the guy I needed to talk to if I was to try and learn from some of his failures. Over dinner that evening he kept us all thoroughly entertained with his story of being rescued mid-Atlantic, a huge reconnaissance aircraft coming out of nowhere and flying right over the boat at very low altitude; a singularly unreal experience after thirty days at sea. The dinner confirmed my intentions; a solo Atlantic row was definitely going to be my next adventure – wife permitting!

Before long I was jumping off the train at Macclesfield, then back home trying to watch telly, still hyper from all the thoughts and feelings whirling around inside. I could sense the tension within Elaine and that burning question I knew she was going to ask. Then it came. 'Well. Are you going to do it then?' Her voice had a tone that I couldn't put my finger on, inquisitive but not angry in any way. I knew what I wanted to say, but how to say it?

'It, er, feels right,' I stumbled. I thought I heard a quiet sigh and rushed to fill the silence. 'But I can't go if you don't want me to; I've got to have your blessing. It's asking a lot, leaving you with the kids...' I trailed off, then feeling horribly guilty added, '...but it won't be longer than three months, I promise.' Another quiet sigh as I stole a glance at her. Elaine gave me that rueful smile of hers: the one that said, 'I'll never stop you from doing what you feel is right but I'll still be worrying about you.' As on my previous Atlantic journey I felt elation and self-reproach. I wanted to go, I didn't want to leave. The silence endured. It seemed right to leave it at that, plenty of time later for more discussion, so I gave her an apologetic shrug and stared at the television, seeing nothing; in turmoil again from torn loyalties. Had she actually said yes or not? I didn't really want to ask.

We eventually went to bed, but I couldn't sleep, my mind spinning as thoughts and ideas passed through without grip or brakes. I needed to slow them down so I could analyse and file them in a logical order; sort of make a list in my mind. Elaine was asleep, her gentle breathing offering a calming backdrop, but I just stared at the streetlight's glimmer through almost closed curtains. All I could see was my Atlantic row, just a tiny flicker of hope now that I reckoned my family was behind me. Part of me wanted to throw the curtains apart and scream that yes, I am up for this challenge! I slipped out of bed, fumbled into a dressing gown and tiptoed down the stairs. I made a brew and sat in front of my computer. If I was going to row an ocean I needed to know about boats, and how to row come to that! I'd had considerable experience of the sea but ocean rowing was a tightly closed book. As an obsessive list maker I needed lots of lists too; that's how I work; make lists and tick boxes to show progress. The foggy mind was clearing; now I could begin my planning; mentally I began to compartmentalise things to do.

I was beginning to discover that ocean rowing wasn't simply a matter of designing a boat and getting on with it. The ORS was an organisation keen to promote the sport and, while it was all very necessary, I didn't want to get involved with the inevitable administration, protocols and politics – I'd got enough of that running my own company. I simply wanted to get a boat and do my own thing. It was my attempt, my challenge. That I was going was now beyond doubt and it made me go cold just thinking about the emotional and logistical feasibility of the challenge. At my core I was committed but sometimes the whole idea felt hazy, as if I was drunk and couldn't sober up. I kept slipping into that clouded feeling where nothing made much sense and I couldn't pinpoint the reason: like having eaten a fabulous meal but still not feeling fully satisfied.

Weeks flew by and while the subject was not part of our conversations at home I continued to identify good contacts with the main players who could help me get to a start line. I spent a hectic couple of days in the South West meeting up with Dorset-based boat builder Charlie Rossiter, who owned an established boatyard and chandlery. We talked designs and costs and at last I felt I was getting somewhere. Charlie felt he could design and build a boat within the one-year timeframe so, buoyed by this, and with Ken Cruchlow from ORS in tow, I dashed to Devon for discussions with Simon Chalk of the Woodvale Challenge Company. Woodvale had taken over rights to the bi-annual ocean rowing race from Chay Blyth, and Simon, with his encyclopaedic knowledge of ocean rowing, stuffed me full of useful information. I was beginning to realise that this sport was dominated by people with a real zest and passion for the oceans and their approach to life was re-igniting the same feelings I'd experienced on my earlier ocean adventure. If I was serious about this row then these people were going to be able to help me find the right boat. It was a mad few days with lots of meetings and a lot of new contacts made. Finally I set off for the long drive back north, agreeing to drop Ken off in Bristol. We had a good, long chat on the way, talking ocean tales, discussing boat designs, equipment and the myriad of things I needed to sort out. But there was still one running sore at the back of my mind. Much of the discussion had been around pairs boats; the sort that Cracknell and Fogle had used; heavier boats with loads of backup support. And the guys I'd met seemed focused on ocean racing. I didn't think I wanted to race. I didn't want to be first; I just wanted to be. To rediscover the achingly beautiful sense of oneness with the waves, the infinite skies, the haunting solitude that is missing from so much of life today. Why would I want to race, forever scanning the horizon for a competitor? That one running sore: Why?

Once I'd dropped Ken off, my mind was reeling but I now had a few hours thinking time to narrow down my choices. Having several choices was good but I knew I was a novice. Had I bitten off more than I could chew? Just how committed was I?

I travelled home with mixed feelings, nothing felt right and my mind was fuzzy. I'd expected it to be easy to get a boat but it was proving very difficult. The plans and boats I had seen were just not doing it. I considered them all and, yes, they excited me in a way but instinctively I knew they were not right and I was just going through the motions. Was this a project destined never to get started?

I had another option and that was to talk with Phil Morrison. Phil is a legend in the ocean rowing boat arena and one of the world's top yacht designers. Formally involved in the America's Cup and other large yacht builds, he is more famously recognised for his designs in the world of dinghy sailing. It would be interesting to see if I could work with him on the same wavelength. I wasn't sure if he'd retired, though I'd picked up an amusing rumour that he worked only when it was raining. I asked Ken if he could organise a meeting as soon as possible.

Back home I reflected long and hard about the whole project; what had happened to date, the people I'd met and what I'd learnt so far about ocean rowing. After a week of emailing and further research I came to the conclusion that if I was going to be successful I needed to get a firm hold of my project and make some progress. I couldn't shake off the feeling that I was being used as a pawn in what seemed a complicated game of ocean rowing chess. I felt pressure to conform, to play to someone else's rules, to be a team player, to be managed. Eventually I trusted the instincts I've lived with all my life. I didn't wish to offend anyone who had helped me thus far but this was *my* project and mine alone. Direct action was needed. I sent Phil an email asking if he would see me alone without any external influences and in March 2007 we met at his Exmouth home. I was energised: I felt sure he would be the right man to help me.

A brisk rain-filled wind greeted me as I stepped out of my car, in stark contrast to Phil's relaxing and hospitable welcome. Over coffee and small talk I glanced around the surroundings; a top shelf full of malt whiskies, presents from his recent sixtieth birthday, photos and paintings of gliders, mountains and picturesque places. There was a warmth to the place and the man; a thoughtful, intelligent guy, soft spoken and with that silver-haired, weathered looked that comes from a lifetime in concert with the sea; a man who instinctively but modestly commanded respect. I knew from the outset that we were going to get on and I think he felt the same. Phil gave me a brief rundown of the history of ocean rowing and I gave him a few sketches of a boat I had in mind, designed specifically for a solo crossing; he'd already given it some thought and made some preliminary drawings too. The conversation felt right and I knew there was a real opportunity here; it was what I had been looking for since the beginning. I wanted a compact, lightweight solo boat and Phil already had ideas and a design, but most of all he had the passion and it was his enthusiasm and emotion that won me over. I was a kid in a sweetshop. Phil Morrison, top man, would be designing my boat, for me, to my spec and with his expertise. Previous fears and anxieties melted away; now I felt a real surge of commitment. My challenge was alive and well and on my terms. We talked technical stuff for several hours then went over to the nearby boatyard and spoke to Jamie Fabrizio, a confident, superb boat builder who I'd briefly met before. Jamie had the same passion as Phil and it was clear that they both wanted to get involved despite Jamie's heavy workload. I could feel the electricity pulse through the boatyard as we discussed the build possibilities. I stood there, in the company of giants, seeing us as three musketeers, all for one and one for all: this was not just about a boat being designed, built and rowed. This was the germination of the seed that would mature; the courtship of three minds to create something more than just a fusion of wood and laminates. As a solo oarsman I had to love the boat, had to feel it, see it grow, grow with it week by week, and I knew Phil and Jamie shared that sentiment. There was, however, a big but: Jamie was still busy and said he would have to think about it. I said my goodbyes, had a final conversation with Phil and then clambered back in the car for the 250-mile slog back up the motorway. The miles slipped away but the smiles remained. I was happy and played some of my favourite tracks to match my upbeat mood. In my heart I knew Jamie would find the time, I could feel the bond between him and Phil. The positive energy was there. Jamie said he would let me know after the weekend. For me it was the only way to get the right boat; Phil could design it, Jamie could build it, and I had the easy bit − I just had to row it.

I sent both Phil and Jamie emails over the weekend and I was sure it was going to happen; I just needed Jamie to agree. Then my mind began to panic. What if Jamie couldn't build it? Who would and what was the impact on my deadline? I had made my mind up that I would be ready to row in January 2008 and that would mean shipping the boat to the Canaries in late November or early December, fully fitted, kitted out and ready to go. It all hinged on Jamie…

I switched the alarm off at 5.30. I've always been a morning person and had a few emails to write before going to work. I hadn't really been sleeping for the last hour anyway, I'd just been lying semi-conscious, thinking shallow thoughts of not really much at all; a sort of time when you're not really fully awake and not asleep; just mumbled dreamy thoughts. It was good to slip into the shower and liven up the brain cells with cascading hot water. I like showers as hot as I can stand them, then finish off with a quick jet of cold water; sometimes it's the only way to get me out. I dressed and crept downstairs to my office. It's a great feeling when everyone is sleeping and you are ready to hit the day full on. I love the morning and in that hour or so before anyone begins to stir I like to work and get a good start to the day. With brew in hand I sat at my desk and shuffled notes and bits of paper to tidy some space while the computer whirred into life. I logged into my emails and the messages streamed through. Junk, junk, junk, Viagra sellers and share tippers, and then one from Jamie popped up. I straightened up in my chair, drew a long breath and held it. This was the mail I had been waiting for; this would decide my fate; Jamie's response. The mouse hovered over the mail icon but I couldn't open it, didn't want the anticipated disappointment, couldn't take the expected setback. I had built my hopes up over the weekend and now I was filled with negativity. I picked up my brew and sipped the hot sweet tea as I gathered my thoughts. Just open the mail, Dave, just open the damn mail! CLICK. My eyes raped the page of words in an instant, brain not quite synchronised with the speed of data being transferred. But within seconds I could see the words among the text...*I will build the boat. I will build the boat.* Yes! Magnificent! Fantastic! I needed to immortalise this life-changing message in print. I read it again, then again. The silly, smug grin on my face got broader, as I didn't quite know how to handle the situation; I reckoned another brew was in order.

I was delighted to have secured the dream team of Phil and Jamie. What bothered me was that *I* might be the weak link. They were masters of their craft; well renowned and revered. I hadn't even rowed a boat before. A little niggle of self-doubt crept in. Were they secretly thinking of me as just another idiot amateur? I didn't think so, but I needed to earn their respect and I wasn't going to get it by doubting myself. I was an accomplished ocean sailor; come on, get a grip, my son, you've got the best team with you and if you think you're the weakest link for success then do something about it. No pressure then.

Commissioning a renowned boat builder was crucial. Jamie Fabrizio had considerable experience of building ocean rowboats and the quality of his constructions was brilliant; very important for the soloist as you need to feel confident that you have the best design and build possible. No one at sea wants to lie awake at night worrying whether the boat will survive the severe stresses of turbulent water, storms and gale-force winds. Energy needs to be saved for the job in hand, not frittered away while nervously anticipating that the next wave will finish you off. Phil and Jamie had had my best interests at heart and this would be reflected in the design and the build of my solo lightweight boat. They had both been talking to several prospective solo rowers that were thinking along the same lines, but nothing had come to fruition. I felt confident that I had the best in the business and hopefully, by the end of the summer, we would have a boat, or at least a constructed shell, which, once fitted out, I could use for trials. Time was not on my side, however, and I continued to fret about getting this project together in time.

I sent Phil further details and sketches of my requirements, but the main issue for me was a design that was compact, light and built for a solo row. I had some other ideas for storage and the fit-out to make it comfortable for me, though that couldn't interfere or compromise the build quality and design. One of the critical issues for me was maintaining a reasonable speed, so Phil had to design a hull that would suit my specifications, with me guaranteeing to keep the fitting-out elements as light as possible. Simply put, the lighter you are the faster you go! For a solo journey I wanted the boat small and compact, so luxuries were out. I couldn't afford to punish myself either as I was planning to take about 60 to 90 days, 100 days at the maximum, a long time to be alone in a tiny boat. So compactness and lightness were what I needed in order to row for twelve to sixteen hours a day. Sixty to ninety days, that was the goal. It was also a promise I had to keep.

I still hadn't quite put my finger on why I wanted to do it. I'd been out for dinner with some friends at the weekend, and when they asked me I couldn't really say. I had a wife and family to look after, and to them it sounded foolhardy and even irresponsible, but I just felt it was something I needed to do. I had crossed the Atlantic before in an eighteen-foot sailboat, so I was no stranger to the sea and its challenge, but this would be very different; this time I wasn't relying on nature's wind in the sails but on my own physical effort. And that was something else I needed to work on if this project was to be a success.

Chapter Two

Birth of a project

I was committed to my new mistress, the dowry was paid and she would be mine: no further courtship was needed.

PROGRESS HAD BEEN GRINDINGLY slow. Drawings seemed to be forever in need of amendment, communication with potential suppliers seemed endless, sponsors seemed indecisive, and choosing the right equipment was a nightmare. The months rolled on and my boat was still at the planning stage. An almost completed plan, admittedly, but the boatyard remained an empty and dusty concrete slab; a birthplace waiting for my baby. This was where Jamie and his logistics-focused wife Emily would convert the plans into a visible, tangible creation; something I could touch and feel: a boat with which I could have some affinity. But when? The whole project felt so near yet still so far away, and it was making me impatient. All my negative thoughts resurfaced; would we have enough time to get it all together? Was I doing the right thing? I worried constantly about the timeframes and contemplated delaying the project for a year. But I couldn't wait another year; circumstances were coming right and might never be the same again. There was no clear, logical defining reason why. It just felt that now was right. Now was my time; selfish, yes, but sometimes there's an inner force that overcomes logic. I knew I wanted, *had* to go, and it needed to be January 2008, just a few short months away.

I phoned Phil who suggested I come down to look at the plans for the hull, get them agreed and signed off. Jamie could then start the build. Phil felt that he would have something ready by 4th May. Into another month, I thought, but at least it felt like some sort of progress. But still I fretted and my lists grew longer. I had only a few months and time was being squeezed. I'd convinced myself that once I'd committed to do the row I didn't want the preparations to drag on, and yet, despite my best efforts, the days were shrinking and still no completed drawings. At some point I'd have to commit to shipping my boat to the Canary Islands, my point of departure. I had a business to run, a project to complete, a family to look after. I was getting severely stressed!

I'd harboured this project for a long time. I suppose the genesis was reading a book years ago by John Fairfax, a British rower and adventurer who became the first person to row solo across the Atlantic in 1969. It took him 180 days. It took me just a few chapters of reading to ignite the dream that perhaps one day I might dare to do the same. The dream was parked in my mind, half-forgotten but never abandoned. I'd filed it under 'one day I'm going to do this' and now that reality was kicking in. I was very clear, however, that I'd need to be in the right frame of mind. I could lock work away in my head though my family would never be far from my thoughts; always there in the depths of my subconscious. I'd read further about other ocean-rowing pioneers and knew that, just like my previous solo Atlantic sailing journey, I was facing both a physical and mental challenge; the possibility of ninety days alone in a hostile yet familiar ocean environment, but this time in an unfamiliar craft. I could be as physically fit as was necessary but without the right mental attitude I wouldn't last more than a few days. Part of the mental attitude was trying not to override my family priorities. If I was looking at a January start for the challenge then I needed to ensure that I spent time with them over Christmas; my plans couldn't involve last-minute preparations and distractions when I should be playing Santa.

The 4th May meeting loomed and I agreed to be at Phil's house in Exmouth for midday. The traffic was the usual Friday madness, and road works around Birmingham didn't help. Once heading south it cleared and the rest of the run was an uneventful slog as the junction numbers counted down and the hours ticked by. I arrived at Phil's house for lunch and was warmly greeted with a pot of steaming hot coffee. His relaxed state seemed to rub off on me and we were soon chatting about progress and what was happening boat-wise.

As we sipped through the first mug of coffee, Phil frenziedly sent his mouse zipping around the computer screen, explaining his reasons for the hull shape. Its length was now just short of the twenty-foot max we had agreed on. On screen she looked good, and as Phil talked me through the design and reasons for it I could feel another lesson in physics was needed in order to understand his comments. I could tell that Phil's main priority was to keep me alive and safe – after all, this was his reputation on the line. I certainly agreed wholeheartedly with the staying alive bit! I had no intention of making the news for all the wrong reasons. It was reassuring though to have it explained, so that I had a full understanding of where Phil was coming from.

We agreed on the hull and decided that at least Jamie could commence construction without delay. I kept all Phil's little sketches and explanations so that I could study them again at a later date. I needed to feel the design coming to life and begin a relationship with my boat; we were going to be very close for a few months and I needed to know her inside out. It might appear strange but I needed that bond, the one a mother always has for her child or that feeling you have when cuddling a puppy and getting a first lick on your cheek. I had no illusions; I was going to be talking to my boat, coaxing her, encouraging her, cursing her. I told myself to be patient, it would come: don't force love onto a set of half-finished drawings. I was committed to my new mistress, the dowry was paid and she would be mine: no further courtship was needed.

Once business was over, Phil and I strolled down to the workshop and discussed the plans with Jamie. He confirmed he could start before the end of May. That affirmation swept over me like a flood. Jamie could get the boat ready for trials before the end of summer at the latest. We chatted through the timescales and he explained the construction materials he'd be using. The boat would be made on a finely cut MDF frame using strips of foam, these would then be coated in a glass-fibre-and-Kevlar matting that would be rolled on with a thin layer of epoxy – it would then be filled and sanded down to get the smooth hull shape. Once complete and fully hardened off the MDF frame work would be removed. I'd insisted on a Kevlar hull, as I wanted it as strong and as light as possible. Jamie's skill was to use the least amount of materials, yet still maintain a solid and strong build. We nodded, agreed and shook hands with enthusiasm. Now to more pressing matters; it was Friday and the pub was open!

We downed a few celebratory pints then returned to Phil's house where his wife Gill had prepared a superb lasagne. We all had a great night and Phil plied us with his top-shelf whiskies once we'd drained all the available bottles of red wine. The night was one of those that you sometimes wish would never end: spontaneous conversations of past and future projects relived and debated, exploits of derring-do more outrageous as the alcohol took effect, but eventually eyelids grew heavy, politeness overcame animated chatter and goodnights were exchanged. I was glad to be a houseguest. I flaked into bed, asleep before my head hit the pillow.

I swear morning arrived early. Gill woke me with freshly made tea, a welcome treat to a mouth that seemed unable to salivate. After a few sips lubricated my tongue I made the inevitable 'never again' promises, but it was all rubbish; alcohol was a master that called his servants often! After a refreshing shower, I made my goodbyes to my genial hosts, then popped across to the workshop to have a last few words with a surprisingly fresh-looking Jamie. With business fully sorted I made an early start back north. The furriness on my tongue and the dull ache in my head were minor irritants. I had my project back on track and my embryonic boat was in safe hands. For the first time in many months I enjoyed a deep well of happiness.

Chapter Three

Gathering pace

As soon as I reckoned I'd thought of everything, something else cropped up

I COULDN'T REALLY TAKE in that I'd finally signed off Phil's hull design. At last I was getting somewhere, and the enormity of the task (and the expense!) was now very real. It's quite remarkable how things become live once ideas leap off the paper and into the workshop. Jamie was ready, all fired up and, with summer approaching, I was impatient to see some early progress. While logically I understood that boat building was a complex and careful process, a part of me remained impetuous, irrationally thinking, 'Come on, get on with it; how hard can it be?' It's a strange sort of feeling. As with any large undertaking it's often hard to encompass it holistically. I have to break it down into small chunks: a bit like the adage how do you eat an elephant? Answer: one mouthful at a time. And that is why I needed to make numerous lists, noting and breaking everything down into bite-size pieces that I could action and deal with. Getting the hull design signed off was one of those items I could now put a tick against and put it to bed. As I watched my sons playing with their Lego models I saw the similarity; get the building blocks in place – piece by piece.

Inertia. There was so much to do I wasn't actually doing much at all. An involuntary freeze frame had taken over my mind. Every time

I added something to a list, another thought popped up that needed including. I was getting to the point that making lists had become the project. I needed to slow my mind down, to take stock and see the bigger picture once again. Hah! Easily said. I had a website to complete, food to source, sponsorship letters to write, costs to absorb, equipment to buy, a personal fitness regime to fit in and somewhere in all that I still had to learn the basics of rowing. I was acutely aware of a time bomb steadily ticking away. My life was being measured in months. I was now into May and had to get the boat finished, completely stocked and ready to be shipped by the end of November at the latest. June, July, August, September, October, November…as I repeated the months I piled the pressure on myself. There wasn't enough time; time was not my friend. What was the urgency? The doubts resurfaced. Why not start the following year, in January 2009? Another year would give me plenty of time to get things sorted. I wrestled with common sense but in the end, as I knew they would, emotion and instinct won the day. I'd made the commitment to January 2008. Back to the lists and the bite-size chunks, Dave. Break it down or *you'll* break down. Break it down into this month and then next month. You can do it; break it down, Dave…

I took refuge in a mug of sweet tea as my pencil danced around the ever-lengthening lists and I felt the panic subside. I took comfort not just in the sugar rush but in the revival of the project. I surmised that as long as I had the boat and the equipment ready for November and I felt good mentally, then I'd be off, and everything else would have to wait. I was still struggling to get a good logistics team around me; lots of people were great at saying they could offer support but inevitably their work and lives took precedence and I was left to sort most things out myself: in a way that suited me as I couldn't take a chance with any of my equipment or supplies. It wasn't a question of distrust; it was possibly a question of survival.

In the back of my mind, since the first glimmerings of an Atlantic row, I'd been wondering about linking up with a charity or foundation that helped young people to develop their interest in sport. My vocational training business was all about offering youngsters opportunities to grow their talents for successful careers, and I thought it would be great to extend that ethos to the world of sports. Trawling through the internet, I chanced upon SportsAid, a charity that supports young budding athletes, so contacted them for a general discussion about joining forces to promote their charity and raise awareness of my project. To my great delight, they immediately saw the potential for a mutually beneficial partnership. What pleased me most was the fact that my adventure now had an additional moral dimension. I could still achieve my own dream and hopefully inspire young people to reach for their own stars. It was a defining moment. I felt a circle had been completed. It was still my project yet I could also give something back to an emerging generation. It's remarkable how much the gesture of giving back can spawn so much personal happiness. As a society we still have so much to learn about what truly matters. SportsAid shared my philosophy and I believed we would create a great partnership. I had some ideas to contribute regarding promotion and, as time was running short, it was wonderful that a charity sponsor had come forward.

The task of approaching sponsors also included organisations for supplies and equipment and most of them seemed interested in the project. Slowly I began to build relationships with companies that could help, but it was time-consuming and quite daunting to identify the vast diversity of items I would need. The list was endless and I shamelessly attempted to wheedle anything and everything I could. Charts, GPS system, compasses, dehydrated foods, protein and energy drinks, waterproofs, base layers and lightweight clothing, emergency beacons, cabin equipment, solar-powered water desalinator, a video camera to record my adventure and…well, there seemed no end to it. As soon as I reckoned I'd thought of everything, something else cropped up; often in the wee small hours when I should have been sound asleep. Full sponsorship has always been nigh on impossible, and as I didn't fall (and still don't) into the category of megastar personality, it was always a case of people I knew to help me get my foot in the door. I had no illusions about getting masses of sponsorship, and every little helped. Concerned at one particular stage about the weight of the boat, I even began to wonder, in a moment of insanity, how much extra weight the sponsors' logo stickers might total. Working on a worst-case scenario I'd already planned to fund most of the project myself, so all discounts and other assistance from companies were a welcome relief from the ever-increasing financial burden. I didn't need convincing that it was worth all the effort, but the tip of the iceberg, the row itself, was hiding a financial chunk of titanic proportions.

On 7th June I received an email from Global Boat Works, Jamie's company. He'd built the frames and had started laying the core strips of foam. My boat was taking shape, my new mistress was no longer a blueprint on Phil's desk but something to admire, something to believe in. Emily had included some photos and where there was once an empty concrete slab now lay the skeleton of a craft that I hoped would take me away, out to a calling ocean and a unique freedom I wanted to experience again. I tried to conjure up an image of myself in my boat, miles from anywhere, but it wouldn't come. I wasn't ready. No matter; it would come soon enough when the seagulls' cries would fade, when the salt would sting my face and the wind would play in my hair and court my spirit. Looking at the photos made me light-headed and pleasantly fuzzy, akin to feeling unreal. My lights were on but nobody was at home; lots going on around me but I wasn't really taking it in. I refocused on the pictures, the first tangible pieces of something material. I could almost smell and even taste the epoxy resin. It was there and yet something held me in check. This was yet another turning point of no turning back. Up until now it had all been 'maybes', but now it was real; a venture crystallised by some MDF board and strips of core cell foam.

I couldn't continue to call her 'the boat'. It had been appropriate when viewed as a blueprint but now that it was a tangible craft she deserved more respect. I approached my fellow-director and suggested that our company might sponsor the hull construction in exchange for naming the boat after the business. This arrangement would significantly help with my costs and provide a unique opportunity to raise the trading profile. And so 'the boat' became *Positive Outcomes*. I was pleased with the agreement as the name had resonance with my project; SportsAid was likewise delighted for similar reasons. I'd recently obtained some local press and radio publicity and was hoping to get some TV coverage, so giving the boat some personality was perfect timing. Appropriate as the name was, it became a mouthful to say, so an affectionate nickname was required. In the teeth of a force eight or the benign calm of a gentle ocean I couldn't talk intimately to a *Positive Outcomes* or even *Pos Out*. Nicknames aren't deliberated; they occur spontaneously and so it was one summer evening, as my mind wandered through the minefield of planning, that a phrase came unbidden. 'One day soon,' I thought, 'I'm going to be away from all this madness. Just me and my boat. *Solo*.' And in that instant I gave my boat her working name. From then on she would be my little *Solo*.

I excitedly showed the beginnings of *Solo* to Elaine but was met with indifference. 'So you're going then,' she frowned. Her response jolted me. Not the reply I'd been expecting, and I suddenly realised how focused and introspective I'd been; too busy and inconsiderate to think about my family's reaction and, not for the first time, I regretted my selfishness. Elaine had never prevented me from following my ambitions, had always been there for me, and she and our sons had a right to expect more. I'm not known for my diplomacy and can be a selfish bugger, but therein lay the conflict. Any massive, complex project like ocean rowing, especially unaccompanied, requires focus, self-belief and almost arrogance to get the job done. But it's not the jaunt it's sometimes depicted to be on television or in the media: a selfish, driven ambition certainly, but it's dangerous, and death or serious injuries are constant companions standing at the shoulder. The trade-off for focus is tunnel vision. Peripherals fade from view, the project becomes all-consuming, and the casualties are one's nearest and dearest. In my case it's never intentional; it's what comes with the territory. To get a project like this to the start line and then row out into a vast ocean takes a certain characteristic trait; a driven individual possessed by the need to complete the task: to achieve personal fulfilment with no thought of failure. The bottom of an ocean is a lonely place and a graveyard already big enough. I could understand Elaine's coldness to what I wanted to do. My constant worry was that she couldn't understand why I was driven to do what I feel I have to do.

The weeks passed by and on 6th July I was off down to the

Exmouth boatyard again. Today was to be a special occasion. It was the turning of the completed hull. Jamie constructed the hull upside down, making it easier to form the shape of the side that sits in the water. Today was indeed going to be special and I was equally keen to learn more about the assembly process.

It was good to get a change from the routine of chasing companies and individuals for sponsorship and supplies, as I had done over the last month, and I was pleased I could have some time off to go and see the construction progress. I was the kid in the sweetshop again, excited as could be with adrenaline surging through my body. I forced myself to pull into the motorway services to grab a coffee and calm down; probably the wrong drink altogether, but at least I'd got out of the car. It was as if I'd found Willie Wonka's golden ticket, but I was the only one who'd entered the competition and only I could win. That word 'win' hung on my tongue. This project wasn't actually about winning in the conventional sense. I didn't want to race across an ocean. No, the winning was about pitting me against me: pushing myself to the limits of self-achievement; biting off a bit more than I thought I could chew. Just for the hell of it, and something deeper I didn't want to ponder; plenty of time for that when I was alone with the beauty of sea and sky. The winning line was a successful crossing; the original adrenaline junkie looking for the next fix. I craved the quiet satisfaction of sitting on a harbour wall halfway across the world, sipping a beer with a quiet sense of satisfaction. Regretful that the row had finished, grateful I was still alive, anticipating the next inevitable adventure. That was winning to me. The Atlantic is a big ocean; mine was an independent challenge, not an organised race with support facilities. This was about me and a boat against the elements, reliant only on each other. I finished my coffee and the philosophising. I felt mentally prepared for the challenge, I would minimise most of the risk by being prepared. Preparation and lists; I would do my best to be as ready as I could ever be.

At last! I stood in the workshop talking with Jamie and Emily. Phil soon joined us accompanied by Peter the electrician, who was there to calculate the electrics and the power needed to run all the equipment. We chatted for a while, then I snuck over to my boat, marvelling at the smooth, dusty hull. A little self-consciously I started to whisper to her, calling her *Solo*, telling her that she was looking fine and that I would take good care of her. I closed my eyes and concentrated as I let my hand run down the freshly sanded hull, trying to get some connection with her; some pulse of static. Some sort of feedback. I needed to know every part of this boat. Man and material would have to come together as one, like the shell of a snail this would be my home, my protection and my life support system for the crossing. She felt good and I let my mind wander to thoughts of tranquil days at the oars, burning sunsets, peace and quiet. I was impressed and felt a bond already. I had a good feeling. I was happy.

I drifted back to the group who were discussing how to turn the boat so that Jamie could start work on stage two, constructing the rest of the build and the topsides. As one we soon turned the hull and sat it in a purpose-built sledge so that she could be worked on safely. Together we checked the measurements against the drawings and discussed a million and one aspects. The conversation was measured but intense with the fine detail agreed, to ensure no hold-ups with the rest of the build. Jamie was aware of the tight schedule and I knew after talking with him that he would get it ready. He'd promised and I believed him. I needed that reassurance to give me the energy to carry on with the next few months, confident there'd be no delay. My life was still in the pressure cooker.

The chatter carried on in the local pub and then into the early hours; a genuine team of wonderful and professional people. I left them later that morning convinced that I would get the best boat possible and, equally importantly, on time. Fully reassured, I left the workshop with more excitement than when I entered. I couldn't get back home quick enough, there was still so very much to do.

The next few months were going to be even harder for everyone involved, either directly or indirectly, and there were times when I worried that so many people were working together just for me to indulge a personal whim. Increasingly, I worried about the real strain this was putting on my personal relationships. The project was consuming my waking hours and even when we were together as a family it was hard to banish it fully from my mind. When talking over domestic stuff with Elaine or playing with the children, *Solo* lurked in the shadows; omnipresent: the damn lists never far away. I also had important responsibilities to my staff and business colleagues. Maybe it was time to book a holiday.

We packed our VW campervan, our lads peering through the windows excited at the prospect of a new adventure, and took the Holyhead ferry over to the Emerald Isle. I've always liked Ireland, especially the southwest coast. Its rugged unspoilt shoreline continually at war with the sweep of relentless winters that have shaped a natural haven filled me with joy at every turn. There's a relaxed feel in the air and life moves at a pace more palatable than I'm used to; a place where I could relax and enjoy some time with my family. It was a much needed break and I realised just how stressed I'd become and how far I'd strayed from the attentive husband and father. The project was not a topic for discussion and definitely off the menu. I was rather relieved that the boys never found a boating lake or demanded a row across the bay.

The fortnight passed all too quickly, and before long we were being buffeted by a stiff south-westerly as the ferry scuttled back into the safety of Holyhead. Holidays are essential but there's nothing like the feeling of getting back to some sort of normality; back to things that are familiar. The boys had missed the TV and their computers and Elaine fancied a long soak in a hot bath and some peace and quiet. Once off the boat, almost immediately the excitement rose in my chest. There'd be a mass of emails waiting to be processed and much to get organised. Elaine was mumbling something about stopping for a bite to eat, and it needed a dig in my ribs to get my attention. Five minutes back on dry land and already the project had reached out and clawed me back. I was now into August.

August. September. October. November. I repeated them again and again in my head. There were only four months, sixteen weeks, before I had to ship the boat. The pressure climbed again. Time was moving at speed and I felt a familiar panic grip my stomach: how could time go so fast, where had the year gone? Clear focus and organisation were now critical or I wouldn't be going anywhere. *Solo* had to be on a trailer, finished and fully loaded with all equipment and supplies and at the docks for the end of November. Panic evolved into fear, dread and the heavy reality that I just wasn't going to have enough time. I felt sick to the core and all my positive thoughts wavered. Surely there was too little time to get everything done and there was still a little matter I'd failed to address. I'd still never pulled a single stroke on an oar.

As we turned the last corner and pulled up on our driveway, I made a pact with myself. I would put all I could into the next few weeks, but if I wasn't fully prepared by the end of September then I would postpone the trip till some other time. I sincerely meant it, but from somewhere distant I heard a wry, hollow laugh…and the faint creaking of a hull.

CHAPTER FOUR

Continued preparation

Every day, ever closer

AS WELL AS SORTING out the boat, equipment, sponsorship and supplies it was important to ensure that the other vital component – me – was in good shape. Although never that unfit, I've always carried a few extra pounds; my mother, ever the diplomat, had always remarked that I was built for endurance, not speed. In one sense I couldn't afford to lose excess weight, and if anything needed to eat lots of junk food to put more weight on: rowing for months on end, all day every day would soon burn off any excess fat. What I wanted was to improve my cardiovascular performance and develop muscle memory for the journey ahead. Every day I pounded the indoor rowing machine for an hour or so and hit the roads with my mountain bike whenever I could. Gradually I was beginning to feel fitter.

Rowing machines and bikes are not perfect simulators for exacting Atlantic conditions, but exercise does have its scary moments. I'd been for a spin on the Cheshire cycle paths in pouring rain and was nearing home; thoughts of a warm shower beginning to filter through the pain. Two hundred yards to go: I was digging in at the rise of a short hill on a single-track road when a high performance car blasted over the brow at breakneck speed, heading straight for me. Survival instinct took over and I dived for the grass verge fearing the worst. The car screeched to a halt then reversed angrily towards me. The door flung open and a suited leg appeared; its owner delivering abuse at the top of his voice. Apparently I'd had the audacity to be on the same road as his penis substitute. There are times when calm, considered measures are not the best solution. To hell with anger management. I stood six feet tall in my bright orange day-glow waterproofs, heaven's liquid dripping from my helmet and nose and none of my 220-pound frame was best pleased. I dropped my bike to the ground, glared balefully and advanced with menace, looking I'm sure like some misshapen, sodden tangerine. I drew breath for the first salvo of invectives when the trouser leg wavered and rapidly withdrew to join its twin. The car revved, spun its rear wheels and sped off, doubtless to find less intimidating victims to terrorise. I reflected that country lanes in our green and pleasant land could easily match a vast ocean for life-and-death situations. At least the chances of ocean rage were slim.

Work had taken a back seat. For quite a few months I'd been strengthening the senior management team to look after the company and taken on several new employees. The task, as ever, in the world of competitive commerce, was to develop the business and continue the steady growth. If truth be told, my enthusiasm for the company had been waning for some time. I needed a break from the responsibilities of managing director and hoped that I could return from my imminent adventure refreshed and reinvigorated. The project was far more interesting to me and a much greater challenge. The logistical pressures and impending deadline consumed my thoughts and the company slipped further from my consciousness. I convinced myself I could hand full control to the new staff and started to concentrate full-time on the project.

While trawling the local media to drum up interest, I'd rather cheekily approached Manchester's Trafford Centre, arguing that my solo crossing would make a great presentation on their main stage in the food hall. To my surprise they were fully behind the idea and agreed to have the boat on show for a weekend, complete with live in-house TV feed, interviews and young people supported by the SportsAid charity. It was a great opportunity, though I wasn't really relishing the idea of doing a public presentation. The centre's marketing manager suggested a weekend in late October, and we started to plan how to make the best of the opportunity.

Sponsors were also becoming more interested, having heard about the project by word of mouth or from my website that was now up and running. I was keen to get sponsorship for the more expensive items such as the electric water maker that Jamie wanted integrating in the boat's construction. At several thousand pounds I was angling for as big a discount as I could in exchange for the manufacturer's logo on the hull. Every piece of kit I needed would be contributing to my survival and, arguably, the water maker was at the top of that list. Without a facility to desalinate seawater my project would be over in a matter of days. The unit would be powered by equally expensive solar panels (though I acquired them at cost) *and* I needed manual backups for anything that would use power. A manually operated water desalinator, while fiddly and time consuming, was still going to cost big bucks, even after a generous reduction; it was still a lot of money out of my rapidly dwindling budget. I had decided that I would back everything up that I classed as important equipment. This meant that anything that would run on solar power had to be capable of operating should the whole unit fail. In fact I'd agreed to two solar power units wired in two separate halves to reduce this possibility, nevertheless navigation, eating, drinking, and lighting were non-negotiable when it came to providing alternatives. Too many rowing attempts had failed through over-dependency on electrical power: I wasn't concerned about losing the use of the satphone or iPod, but for everything else it was yet again a case of covering all the bases with detailed preparation.

In common with many people I'm odontophobic. This is the posh way of saying I'm scared of dentists: actually, more pathologically petrified than scared. After a few visits as a child I didn't visit a surgery until my early twenties, preferring the physical pain and prolonged mental suffering, my imagination racking up the painometer to infinity and beyond. I can weather a gale in mid-Atlantic with no more than unease, but the thought of trying to extract one of my teeth with a pair of rusted, salt-encrusted pliers at sea was a nightmare too far. In late August I told myself I was a tough northern lad, not some soft Jessie, made an appointment and succumbed to my fate; the treatment being for some root canal work. To be honest the treatment and dentist were excellent and slowly I became more and more tolerant as he worked his magic, but it didn't entirely stop the fear. I focused on the surgery ceiling, willing myself to think about my coming adventure in little *Solo* – and the promised assurance that my pliers would stay firmly in the toolbox for the duration of the crossing.

At the end of August I again travelled down to Jamie's workshop. Phil was away but I wanted to spend some time with the boat, as the cabins, deck and topside work were close to finishing. It gave me the opportunity to compare the blueprints with the final construction and get a sense of how the project was shaping up. I'd agreed with SportsAid that the boat would be completed and ready for display in the London Hilton Hotel for the annual charity dinner on 9th October. A top-drawer event with over 700 distinguished guests and celebrities including four-times Olympic gold medallist Matthew Pinsent. We had thirty-nine days left to get the boat fully fitted, complete and on display in London. It was excruciatingly easy to panic and switch priorities to the gala event, but that would mean compromising the boat and my safety. What an ignominious epitaph that could read – 'His priority was beauty over function'. I put it out of my mind: if it wasn't ready then it wouldn't go: I wasn't going to compromise the build for a night of glitter and glamour. I'd also agreed that the Trafford Centre weekend show would be two weeks later. How on earth was I going to fit all this in and test the boat and all the equipment? I had to put it out of my mind. The weekend with Jamie would be spent assisting where I could; I wanted to help, not put him under more pressure.

I was greeted in the workshop with a hot coffee and one of Emily's baked bean and cheese toasties, a dish she had come across in her student days. I can wholeheartedly endorse this basic meal as an inspiration; nothing fancy, just simple ingredients transformed into a delightful dish.

With bean juice running down my chin I drew in the sight before me: my boat; my *Solo*; numbed speechless as my eyes attempted to absorb all the detail and relay it back to my brain in double-quick time. Jamie and Emily just stood there with smug grins on their faces. Emily had held back some photos so I'd be surprised by the progress when I arrived. It worked. I continued to munch down the molten cheese and scalding beans in an effort to express myself, but it was futile. The toasty was winning so I simply stared wide-eyed for a few minutes; talking would come later. I was content just to look, marvelling at how strips of core cell foam and plywood had been transformed into something that was a boat. And what a fine boat she was, dainty and ladylike with lovely clean lines and angles, but strong and safe too. If she looked this good now how impressive would she be in another month?

I couldn't thank Jamie enough for the skill that was apparent in the quality of the build, I was actually stunned as I checked and rechecked every detail. Nothing was rushed or less than 100 per cent perfection. She was a joy to behold. Jamie was a true craftsman and had built her with such passion and pride. Just beautiful.

I sat in the cockpit for an hour or so getting a feel for her, checking the layout and how the designs had been transferred into material form, so different now that they'd leapt from the page. As I sat in the cabin I tried to envisage how it would feel to spend nights alone, locked away in a space barely big enough in which to sit and lie down: small but womblike; a sense of safety and snugness about it and adequate for my needs on the ocean; somewhere to get dry and go to sleep. I also knew from bitter experience that this pleasant aroma of newness would all too soon be replaced with the fetid, dank stench of wet clothes and my unwashed, salt-ridden body.

We discussed and agreed some minor changes to the plans, which would be checked with Phil when he returned from holiday and cleared up a few niggles that he sorted on the spot. Jamie confirmed he was on target and if all went to schedule then she would be ready for me to put her on the trailer and take her away. We agreed that date; Friday 5th October. Five weeks' time.

I went down again a couple of weeks later to make sure everything was on target and deal with the inevitable little issues. I'd been that busy with the logistics of the project that I hadn't really thought that much about the actual crossing. I knew what it had been like sailing out on my earlier transatlantic journey, but rowing would be a completely different experience. Once more I sat in the cabin and reflected on the emotions I could expect to feel on leaving the safety of harbour for the emptiness that is a vast ocean. Alone and with no reliance on the wind or the chattering of a sail? Within days I'd lose sight of land and then it would just be me and *Solo*. Reliant on each other for the next 3,000 miles, doing battle with whatever nature intended to throw at us, but hopefully sharing some great moments too. It was a moment I was looking forward to and dreading in equal measure. I knew that the first pull on the oars would be the hardest bit, not of just the journey, but the whole project: the elemental feeling of letting go of that final tie with land, civilisation, friends and family; coiling up the mooring rope and stowing it away. Picking up the oars, a few strokes, then clear of the safety of the harbour I would be voluntarily cast adrift. Alone. I felt the hair on my neck prick up and my pulse quicken. Reality was sinking in, the row was on schedule and D-day was edging closer. The old familiar doubts began to nibble at my consciousness, resurfacing with increasing intensity. Could I actually do it? Could I let go of that line, that umbilical cord that ties us all to comfort and certainty? Once I'd picked up the oars there would be no going back, my pride wouldn't let me for a start…but what if I couldn't do it? What then? I hadn't been to sea for over a decade. I felt a cold shiver of fear, once more wondering whether I'd bitten off more than I could cope with. Most people I'd met had been fascinated as to how I would deal with the constant physical strain while studiously avoiding asking about the mental strain, but I was again questioning the latter. My body would cope if my mind was fit enough to tell it to. The game had started. I had the end goal in my sights and had to dig deep and focus, to condition my mental state to the expected crossing.

My reverie was interrupted by the sight of Emily's head popping through the hatch cover and into the cabin. 'Fancy another brew, Dave?' she smiled.

'Fancy a row with an old sea dog?' I replied. 'Keep treating me this well and I'll insist on you coming with me.' I dismissed the negative thoughts; I could work on them later. Now was the time to enjoy the boat and make sure everything was in place so that Jamie could crack on and keep to his tight deadline.

After a long day of working and discussion, the three of us headed off to the pub for a few drinks. I'd promised Jamie and Emily a curry to thank them for all their efforts. They'd been putting in some long hours to make sure the schedule was achievable. It was difficult to express but I sensed that my project had been more than just an ordinary job of work to them, more than just a contract to be completed. Their enthusiasm and interest would be ingrained in the whole fabric of the boat and their spirits would be with me, friendly ghosts watching over my endeavours. I couldn't articulate that feeling over a pint and a meal but I think they knew how much I'd valued their friendship and commitment, and that was sufficient. The evening went well; we discussed the boat and the project well into the night, before finally retiring for some well-earned sleep.

The next day we were all back in the workshop following up the practicalities of issues we'd discussed the previous night. Some worked, some didn't, but it was great to be back with my boat. The bond was strengthening and I was starting to enjoy the prospect of crossing an ocean. The more the boat edged towards completion, the nearer my dream, this ambition, this escapism, was to a beginning – ever closer every day.

I said my goodbyes to Jamie and Emily and headed home. I'd promised Elaine that I wouldn't be late back and I was anxious to keep to that pledge. She was slowly either accepting the fact that I was leaving her and our sons or was putting the whole venture out of her mind. It rarely came into our conversations, the elephant in the room. If I did mention it, the atmosphere chilled and strained and had to be handled with care. It wasn't an easy situation for her; I understood that, but I'd made my decision to see the project through and I had to live with the consequences. Torn in two again: the beckoning finger of a special personal freedom and the logic of important responsibilities. No middle way. One or the other.

I was convinced that *Solo* would be ready for shipping; now I had to get myself ready, together with all the other thousands of details, supplies and equipment. The logistics were generally fine, but was I? For a few months I'd been suffering from serious backache and had put it down to increased exercise and the rowing machine, but instinctively something didn't feel right. I decided to give it another month and if it still wasn't right I'd go to a specialist. I pre-booked some appointments with the chiropractor to ease my conscience, but I just hoped the pain would go away: I was already sufficiently stressed; last-minute cancellation was not an option.

CHAPTER FIVE

She's mine at last!

Bubbling with animated expectancy, savouring the moment

SEPTEMBER WAS SLIPPING BY in a flash; I've never known a month go by so quickly. My diary was full of appointments and notes. The project was gathering momentum and I felt pleased that, while the pace was frantic, I'd generally got things under control. I loved the buzz that was being generated. This is what I'd wanted. This is what I'd been working towards this past year. This was great. So, deep down, why didn't I feel it?

I'd just turned over the page in my diary to Monday 1st October, and laid before me was the new week's actions. 'Friday 12 o'clock Exmouth' caught my eye immediately: 'collect boat'. There it was; probably still being worked on even as I read the entry. The enormity of what I'd been planning and working towards hit me again and I felt the familiar acid lurch in my stomach as the old doubts and self-questioning momentarily surfaced. Was I really capable of this challenge? Physically, my back was giving me hell and had not improved, though I was hiding the pain from everyone, popping the painkillers when it was too agonising to sleep. But it was also my mental state with which I wasn't comfortable; constantly questioning my self-belief; subconsciously nagging at my brain with questions, doubts, anxieties. I'd experienced the same fears before my solo sail across the Atlantic in the '90s and knew they were rational and inevitable, but this time I was sure they were deeper; far more deep-rooted than any eager anticipation to get started. Now in my forties, was my mid-life crisis real and was it kicking in? Ought I to call the whole thing off, postpone it or do something less adventurous with the boat? Had I fully considered the impact on my family, my work – even my life? My transatlantic sail had been accomplished after several years' experience in coastal and deepwater environments. This time around I still hadn't rowed my boat – hadn't rowed any bloody boat!

The next few minutes were hazy and slow. I was facing a diary full of lists and things to do, and yet I sat bewildered, vacant, motionless, wax-like in a trance of overload. Emotions and reasoning not in check, surrounded and overcome by a haze of negativity. The moment passed. Small doubts lingered but I shrugged them off and got down to planning the week, some inner strength returning. I had a sudden insight into to what I would have felt if I'd really called the project off – and I didn't like it. I would hate myself forever and never be able to look in a mirror again. I would be shamed, my self-esteem would disappear and I'd never know whether I'd have succeeded or not. To pull out now was a route to despair I couldn't, wouldn't face. Come on, you bugger, it's only a mid-life crisis; get over it!

What I needed was the ever-ready solution to all those times when things were burdensome. I needed a walk in the hills to clear my head, some downtime from the project. Living on the edge of the Peak District gives me instant access to a natural beauty I never tire of, and within a few short minutes I was out of my front door and heading into the hills. A crisp day greeted me; an autumnal edge that took my soul to the blue sky and the promise of a high moorland trek: silent, save for sheep, birds and the wind. A distant tractor crawled effortlessly across the landscape and the brooding hills beckoned. I took a deep breath. Life was good. I would look forward to a different landscape in just a few months; a seascape actually, but the same emotions would be stirred again. I heard the sound of freedom in the wind, tasted it, longed for it. I would row the Atlantic and re-conquer my life's fears. Deep down I knew I could do it. All was well.

Four and a half hours later I was back at my desk, exhausted and hungry but satisfied that I was now back in control, ready for this very special week. Collecting my boat was just a few days away and now was a time for celebration and tying up loose ends.

Friday arrived all too quickly and at midday I was still at my desk. I'd been finalising arrangements for both the London SportsAid Ball and the Trafford Centre weekend, and time had run away with me. By mid-afternoon plans had been taken as far as they could; I was ready for the off. Friday afternoon wasn't the ideal time to be heading south but I didn't care, the destructive thoughts that I'd had on Monday were well and truly put to bed and I'd had a great week pushing things on, giddy with excitement at the prospect of bringing *Solo* home. At long, long last she was finally ready for her purpose. It had seemed years since we'd started the preliminary discussions, then the designs, the tight deadlines and the numerous trips down to Jamie's boatyard. I would genuinely miss these drives down south. Any romantic thoughts about them, however, were soon brought to a sudden halt, as was the traffic on the M6. Already a crawling ribbon of vehicles, and I was still less than an hour from home. What the hell, I'd waited long enough for this day; another few hours of anticipation wouldn't matter. My face kept its smile and I was happy.

I arrived in Exmouth too indecently late to rush off and see my boat, so after a few pleasantries and a mug of hot sweet tea it was off to bed. The occasion reminded me of Christmas Eve as a child, bubbling with animated expectancy, savouring the moment but not wanting it to last too long. The seven-hour slog down south had been exhausting, so within minutes I'd drifted off into a deep and well-earned sleep.

At eight o'clock next day I was outside the workshop and impatiently awaiting Jamie. The morning was cool with the sun yet to have any warming effect, but a clear spell was forecast with no rain. Come on, Jamie, I've got a boat to drool over!

He soon arrived, and with the workshop open and a freshly made brew in hand we discussed the boat and some of the final jobs he'd completed. There wasn't a lot left to do other than get her on the trailer and take her home. She looked a treat, sparkling in the sunshine and immaculately finished. Most of the SportsAid and other logo stickers had been applied and added a splash of colour and professionalism. Deep blue hull, dazzling white topside, polished teak trim, gleaming black oars; this was a real labour of love and surely a craft destined for greatness. She was no longer just a boat, now she was my little *Solo*, formally known as *Positive Outcomes* in recognition of my company's support. It suited her. I certainly hoped the crossing would be a positive outcome! I swelled with pride. If last night had felt like Christmas Eve then today certainly was Christmas Day. I devoured her sleek looks with eyes and hands, grinning like an idiot, Jamie trying hard not to smirk. Who was he kidding? He was as chuffed as I was.

Emily arrived with electrician Pete plus Phil, all willing to help get her on the trailer. Jamie had hired a chap with a Land Rover to pull her out of the workshop around the beach and up to the car park where I would hook her up and take over. I was in the VW camper and it wouldn't have coped with the sand. There was a moment of anxiety as we winched her onto the trailer, but Phil took control in his calm manner and it wasn't long before she was secured and ready to go. Now was a bittersweet moment and I felt a lump in my throat. I'd wanted this day to come for so long but now it had arrived I was having to say goodbye to all the experiences I'd treasured these past months. Phil, Jamie, Emily and Pete, individually wonderful people and a fantastic team with which to work. I'd keep in touch, but from a distance, so it was a brief goodbye, a promise to take care of my (our?) boat, a final check of the towing gear, then I pulled away from the boatyard for the last time. They waved into the rear-view mirror, reducing specks of friendship standing by what was again a bare concrete slab.

I headed off north, stopping at every opportunity to check that the boat was secured and that the new trailer was holding up. It was hard to ignore the glances from other people, good to be taking her home but not quite believing she was mine. Before long I was pulling into my drive and parking up. Elaine and the boys came out to see her for the first time. The kids explored and rushed around it, sitting in the cabin, pretending to be on the ocean and sliding the seat on its runners. I looked at Elaine and I could tell she was surprised at how good the boat looked. I didn't think she was fully convinced I was doing the right thing but perhaps it was a small step along the way to reconciliation.

CHAPTER SIX

Stuck in Mayfair

I sat with my head in my hands, the only consolation a large glass of red wine

I'D BARELY SLEPT A wink since bringing *Solo* home, yet I was up early the next day, anticipating several frantic hours of preparations getting her ready to be trailered down to London in time for the SportsAid dinner, just a few days away. I rushed hither and thither, feeling like Buttons, proud to be taking my Cinderella to the ball but desperate to ensure it didn't turn out like a pantomime. As the boat would take pride of place at the event I'd taken the precaution of travelling to London a month earlier to check the arrangements and make sure we could get her to the first floor of the Hilton Hotel. Wouldn't it be embarrassing, I'd thought, if we were to go all that way down to find she wouldn't fit through the doors?

I'd enlisted the assistance of my nephew Gary to help with logistics, provide the necessary muscle and share the long drive south into the heart of the city centre. We drove through the night arriving at the Hilton just after five o'clock. We were under instruction to get the boat in the service lift and up to the first floor before six, as many deliveries would be arriving throughout the day, the events company wanting the boat in place before all hell was unleashed. I eased myself out of the campervan and stretched, looking upwards at the imposing storeys of brightly lit concrete and glass; a cloudy steel-grey sky edging aside the darkness of pre-dawn.

'Good morning,' I called to the night manager leaning against the back of the loading bay, 'how do I get the boat up to the first floor?' Customer service was clearly not at the top of his agenda and an already surly grimace spread further across his face. 'Jobsworth' was written all over him as he denied knowing anything about our arrival or tight schedule. Gary, being an intimidating member of the Paratroop Regiment, was all for a bit of strong-arm tactics but I bit my lip, smiled and pleaded the importance of the occasion, telling the officious manager how vital it was to get my boat into his lift, how it was an essential part of a charity event for young people and (silently) how much Gary was looking forward to punching his lights out.

'Ten minutes,' I said. 'Just ten minutes and we're out of your way.' Power play over and convinced he'd won the exchange, Jobsworth relented and jerked a dismissive thumb in the direction of the lift. 'Ten minutes,' he echoed. 'I've got important deliveries coming in.'

Gary and I manhandled the boat from the trailer and squeezed it into the lift, a huge six-by-three-metre box, scratched and beaten by years of hard treatment at the hands of crews shifting tons of equipment for countless functions. Large as it was, the available space rapidly shrank as we puffed and strained to get *Solo* in with just inches to spare. We set her up near the bar area by the entrance to the function room where she assumed a regal air, as if made for the moment, gleaming immaculately in the spotlight and awaiting the inevitable attention. I couldn't help a wry smile, thinking how different she'd look after a few months of heavy seas, encrusted barnacles and scant regard from me. But now was *her* time, a time to woo and impress. She would be the star; I'd just be the guy going along for the ride. A final tweak to the display, and Gary and I headed off for a well-earned breakfast of bacon and eggs – the ideal great British fare with which to revive our flagging energy levels. Satiated at last and with fatigue kicking in, we headed back to the campervan to manage a few hours' sleep in the car park. As I hunkered down

I felt the old familiar backache flaring up again, a niggle I'd had for much of my life, but now it was getting worse, much worse. Need to watch that, I thought, as I drifted off to sleep, rowing and bad backs were not good bedfellows.

That afternoon I headed in to the Hilton through the front door and met Elaine in the overnight room we'd booked. I'd treated her to a first-class train journey down to London and we were soon resplendent in our formal attire. That had been a job and a half at best. Neither of us is 'dressy' but as this event was high status it had been necessary for me to acquire a dinner jacket and black bowtie, and I wanted Elaine to look her most glamorous in something in which she'd feel comfortable. I'd forgotten how difficult it was to find the 'right' posh frock; rowing the Atlantic was going to be a simple affair by comparison. A few weeks earlier we'd popped over to York for the seemingly easy task of choosing an outfit. Hundreds of miles walking the High Street, dozens of 'well it's nice but I'm not sure', endless 'what do you think to this?' and the same old answer: 'You look fine, it's great, just buy it.' And then, hours later, the final decision: 'I think I like the one we first saw this morning.' And like it we did, and gorgeous she looked as we made our way through the hotel corridors to the VIP suite.

The first impression as we walked through the doors was one of amazement. A vast, opulent room stretched before us, endless round tables set for dinner, the whole affair bathed in a purple hue. Eight hundred people chatted in small groups, eating canapés and making small talk. Males of various shapes and sizes preened like an army of penguins while the more colourful females shimmered and swanked, constantly glancing furtively at the competition, with occasional worry lines appearing at the prospect of someone wearing the same creation. The second-best-looking lady was by the bar. *Solo* gleamed and glistened in the spotlights as guests buzzed around her. She looked tiny in the huge banqueting suite, her strength hidden by a look of fragility, as if aware that this was not her chosen environment. I was apprehensive and proud. Proud of my wife, my boat and the fact that I'd made it to this point despite all the worry and tribulations along the way. We made our way across to *Solo* to parry the inevitable questions that would come my way – where are you rowing from, where to, how long will it take, what will it be like, what's this for, what's that for, what training are you doing, what happens if things go wrong, what will you eat? Occasionally I just longed for the quietness of the ocean and when asked 'Why are you doing it?' a part of me just wanted to say, 'I'm a selfish bugger, there are times when I need space just to be me.'

But of course I didn't, it was a great occasion and the biggest initial shock was in realising just how many showbiz and sporting celebrities were in attendance. At least fifty Olympians including Linford Christie, Kriss Akabusi, James Cracknell, Tessa Sanderson and Dame Tanni Grey-Thompson DBE. It was hard not to be overawed as so many famous people approached the stand, and when a certain Matthew Pinsent approached, sat on the boat and engaged me in long conversation, I was in disbelief. Here was a man whose passion was rowing, a real-life hero of mine, yet genuinely interested in my preparations and fascinated by the boat design: a true gentleman and very encouraging.

'You're mad,' he said, shaking my hand. 'You do know you're mad, but you have my very best wishes.'

Onto the stage strode our compère for the evening, GMTV presenter and news anchorman Andrew Castle, himself a former professional tennis player. His role was to introduce guests who would present awards to various people for their contributions to the SportsAid charity and to laud the efforts of determined youngsters who would be the sportsmen and women of the future. And then, oh crikey, on the giant screen behind him appeared a video I'd made of *Solo* being constructed, training on Rudyard Lake and a few pre-recorded interviews. The spotlight fell on me as Andrew announced my project and partnership with SportsAid, echoing the earlier remarks by Matthew that I must be mad to make the attempt. He generously mentioned the promotional weekend at the Trafford Centre in Manchester, then a microphone was thrust in my hand and, to much applause, I had to stand, face my peers and thank everyone for their support. The whole thing felt like hours but probably lasted less than five minutes; I could feel the sweat soaking and cooling my shirt. I hated the attention, but recognised the importance of the event. I felt I was there under false pretences, a bit of a fake. What right did I have to be in the company of these real sports personalities who live and breathe their sport in the hunt for that sometimes elusive gold medal? My gold medal would be to survive and get to the other side, recognising it would be no hundred-metre sprint, more like many marathons day after day, a real effort to keep body and mind together. I sat down as the applause died away and the focus moved elsewhere. I toyed with my meal, thoughts fragmenting, a 'celebrity' for a few seconds, but the real celebrities had seemed to have genuinely recognised my endeavours. Perhaps this was their way of acknowledging that they understood the core of what I was attempting and the personal impact it would make. Perhaps I wasn't a fake. I relaxed a little and the chicken dinner seemed to taste better.

We had a great night with many messages of good luck and support; having the boat there certainly helped raise the profile of the project and the SportsAid organisation. All too soon it was midnight and guests slowly started to make their way home. Elaine and I were staying in the hotel but Gary had offered to take the boat back home that night so we began to collect the gear together and prepared *Solo* to go back in the service lift. The only guys left were the riggers who'd built the stage, installed the sound and lighting and set up the decorations. Clearly they'd done this a thousand times before and the organised way they were packing up the mass of gear was impressive. We waited our turn as they loaded up the lift, wedging one of their large metal boxes against the open door. Suddenly, without warning, the lift started to descend. To an almighty sound of crunching steel, the lift door buckled and semi-ripped off, rendering the lift unusable. It shuddered to a halt a few feet down as the electrical system was destroyed. The maintenance manager was called, shook his head and declared it to be a write-off.

The earlier euphoria flooded away. I sat with my head in my hands, the only consolation being a large glass of red wine on the table before me. The maintenance manager said it would take about four to six weeks to repair the lift, the entertainment director said the boat would have to go as the function room would need to be readied for the next event. Stress and tiredness were beginning to build. All I could think of was the tight schedule ahead. Trials on Rudyard Lake, the Trafford Centre weekend just days away and myriad details to organise. Things were going wrong and panic was welling up as I stared hopelessly at Elaine. What do we do now? I took the easy option and recharged my glass as the hustle and bustle of the huge clear-up was going on around me. Before long the hotel manager was huddled with his staff trying to resolve the problem. The rigging company guys were going mad as dozens of heavy boxes had to be manhandled down awkward flights of stairs, and things were not fitting down easily. It was now past one o'clock and there still seemed lots of problems and no solutions. Finally, I'd had enough so went to see the hotel manager myself and explained that I needed my boat out of the hotel as much as he did and what were we going to do? As he searched for a reply the safety and maintenance manager, who'd been on the phone to the lift engineer, came across to report his findings. After assessing the damage to the door, they felt there was a slim possibility that we could remove the door, put the boat inside and then manually release the lift and wind it down. There would just be the one opportunity as the lift could only be wound down manually with no chance to repeat or reverse the operation. It was the chance I needed; the only chance I had. Within the hour we had her safely deposited in the lift and after few anxious minutes she was at last on the ground floor, secured on the trailer and ready for home. I thought of all the celebrities I'd met just a few hours earlier, all tucked up, sound asleep and blissfully unaware of the travails of the working classes! With great relief I waved goodbye to Gary and headed off for my hotel room and a stiff nightcap: a long, eventful, nerve-racking day in many ways, but still a wonderful occasion. I'd been privileged to meet some heroes of mine and had had an anxious 'up-lifting' experience. Life was certainly never dull.

CHAPTER SEVEN

Positive outcomes

Spotlights, balloons and all the frippery of a glitzy show

I'D BEEN WORKING FLAT out since returning from the SportsAid bash and most of the equipment and supplies I needed were either on order or stored in my garage. My tick lists were coming together and even my overarching 'to do' list was getting progressively shorter.

The Trafford Centre promotion weekend was only a few days away so I needed to focus on that, get it out of the way then launch and moor the boat at Rudyard Lake reservoir, leaving it there until it was shipped to La Gomera. That way I would have all of November to trial the boat, get to know her foibles and give us both a thorough testing, leaving sufficient time for last-minute adjustments. Looking back it seems remarkable that even at that eleventh hour I'd still not rowed a boat on water. My landlocked rowing machine had been in daily use to build up stamina and strength but it was a far cry from the real thing. Occasionally the thought flickered through my mind that there was still a possibility that, despite all the time, energy and money I'd committed to this project, I might find I couldn't actually row a boat at sea. What a great headline that would be; wouldn't my sponsors be thrilled! The thought evaporated instantly. I hadn't come this far to fail through a mere technicality.

The Trafford Centre is a huge cavernous building and a monument to retail therapy. A cornucopian emporium surrounded by vast acres of car parking, its hallowed halls permanently teeming with people anxious to overburden their credit cards and lighten their wallets. From a burger to a bath, a dress to a diamond, the place oozed choice as families, couples and individuals rushed or strolled through the tempting array before them. All I needed them to do was to take their eyes from the tills for just a few moments and grab their attention.

I met Alison and her mall entertainment team who took me to the spacious arena that was the Orient Food Court. Also there were Lynne Baird, regional development manager, and several of her staff from SportsAid. A few of my own employees had also volunteered to help, and together we transformed the main stage into what seemed to be the Dave Clarke spectacle. In reality SportsAid was using my challenge to launch its fundraising activity in the North West, so that the money could be pumped back in to support the development of the region's talented young athletes. Centre stage of course was *Solo*, taking the limelight again, shameless hussy that she was turning out to be. Around her were promotional banners, literature and information about SportsAid and my imminent row. Making the exhibition more interactive and dynamic, Dan Hetherington arrived from British Rowing, the national body co-ordinating the development of the sport and the training of rowers at all levels. Dan was a regional coach and brought along several rowing machines linked to a computer screen, the intention being to encourage the public to try them out and compete in virtual racing competitions. Completing the line-up was Sport England with their freebies, banners and display boards busily promoting the benefits that could be had from sport in general. All in all it was turning out to be quite a colourful and professional-looking affair. Hot spotlights, balloons and all the frippery of a glitzy show completed the effect, and before long it was time to kick-start the event. It suddenly struck me just how many high-level individuals from national sports bodies had turned out to promote their own organisations and support my project, all because of my crazy ambition: quite remarkable how random and unpredictable life could be. A switchback set of twists and turns, chance meetings and decisions taken that opened up new avenues. It had all led to this overture before the main event. I looked around the noisy arena, now jam-packed with onlookers, diners and my family and supporters. A simple idea to row a boat had taken me to a showcase event in a massive food hall: astonishing and pretty scary. I glanced at my watch. The waiting was over. It was time to be a 'star' again.

I'd thought the Hilton Hotel event to be nerve-racking in front of 700 people. Then, I'd spoken by a bar to small groups and individuals and had had just a few moments of thanking a quiet and attentive audience. That had been enough to drench me in sweat but as I climbed up on the Trafford Centre stage I felt the now familiar panic beginning to surface again. The stage was probably only two or three feet above the main concourse but it felt like the summit of Everest. Just me in front of at least 2,000 noisy people, some more interested in what they were eating but nevertheless glancing in my direction as I clambered inelegantly into their line of vision. I could not have been more uncomfortable if I'd been stark naked. Wotcha doing, Dave? This is not your scene.

By way of small recompense I was quickly joined at the gallows by Yemi Sawyerr, a professional presenter. He was going to compère and host the event and couldn't have been more different from the quaking shell I recognised as me. A mid-twenties ebullient black guy with an easy smile and engaging banter (bloody hell, I could have hated him!). He launched into a great build-up of who I was, what I'd done, what I was hoping to achieve and the link with SportsAid. He painted a heroic picture of life alone on the stormy seas: according to him I was inspirational, courageous, determined (bloody hell, I was beginning to like him again) and then he went and spoilt it. He turned to me, pointed one expansive hand towards *Solo* while thrusting the microphone in my direction and said, 'Well Dave, it's a great boat, can you tell me something about her?' As the last letter rolled from his vocal cords the fear factor shot into me like a reddened poker. My mouth stopped producing saliva and felt as if several dry Weetabix had been shoved in to replace it. Dry mouth and wet back as an instant eruption of frightened sweat-gland activity caused seepage into my shirt. Time froze: everything seemed to slow down then stop. I was suddenly conscious, as from an out-of-body perspective, of piercing spotlights, people looking at me, and the horrible thought that I couldn't answer Yemi's question. My memory emptied itself and refilled with panic. I could still hear that last 'r' rolling from Yemi's vocal cords. How can a few milliseconds last so long?

Feeling horribly foolish, I smiled weakly, summoned up some moisture from somewhere, stared at the mic like a fool and stumbled some idiotic response, all the while desperately trying to drag some semblance of confidence and authority back to the proceedings. Under Yemi's expert guidance the ordeal waned and I gradually got up to speed, eventually daring to admit that I'd sort of enjoyed the experience. Sort of.

The weekend was busy and unreal. In between interview sessions with Yemi I took questions from shoppers who were looking over the boat, encouraged individuals to have a go on the rowing machines and generally helped promote SportsAid and raise awareness of my ocean challenge. It was particularly fulfilling to speak to youngsters, explain that I was not a hero or a celebrity but just like them, an ordinary guy from a normal background who had an ambition I wanted to fulfil. If I could do this, so could they. I like to think that in some small way a youngster might have walked away with aspirations beginning to stir. I'll never know. Between stage sessions I did a couple of ninety-minute book-signing sessions in Selfridges, putting a signature to the flyleaf of *An Ocean Away*, an account of my previous successful Atlantic crossing under sail. It felt very strange to see copies of the book appear before me, felt a little fraudulent but nevertheless I enjoyed the fleeting impression of fame. Back on stage I was delighted to welcome to the event seventeen-year-old Olivia Oakes, one of the UK's rising rowing stars and tipped for a world-class future. Adding glamour to the occasion, charming and much more at ease than I was, she chatted easily with onlookers and willingly pitted herself against the mainly teenage lads who fancied beating her at the rowing machine races. She had the confidence of youth and the motivation to be the best that she could be, a real ambassador for Britain and a positive role model for millions of young people in this country.

1. *Above: Jamie on the left and Phil on the right in the workshop.*
2. *Below left: Jamie fixing the strips of core cel foam on the MDF frame.*
3. *Below right: Hull filled and ready for sanding.*

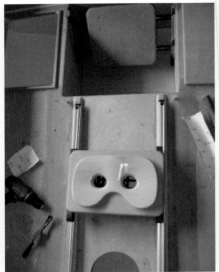

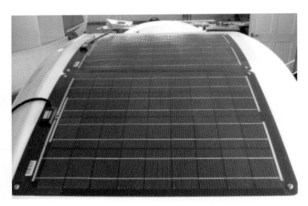

4. Above left: Checking measurements.

5. Above right: Fitting the rowing seat.

6. Left: Fitted solar panels.

7. Below left: Water desalinator built into the construction of the boat.

8. Below right: Control panel for the electrics.

9. Facing page, above: A final pose in Jamie's workshop.

10. Facing page, below: On the trailer and ready to go.

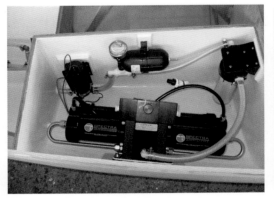

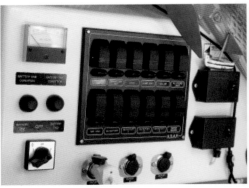

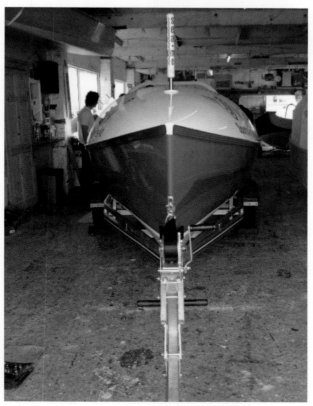

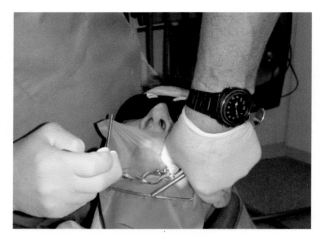

11. *Left: Fighting my fear of the dentist with some early morning root canal work.*

12. *Below: Sir Mathew Pinsent and I at the SportsAid Dinner.*

13. *Right: Live interview for BBC Breakfast Radio as the sun comes up.*

14. *Enjoying the banter on stage with Yemi at the Trafford Centre.*

15. *Visitors of all ages get a close-up look at Solo.*

16. Left: Dan from British Rowing with a young visitor keen to learn.
17. Below left: Getting ready to roll Solo.
18. Below right: Solo at the point of no return!
19. Bottom left: The lads get wet and I'm seeing stars in the cabin.

20. *Solo dwarfed by Miguel's fork lift truck, La Gomera.*

21. *At the moorings in La Gomera just a few hours before setting off.*

22. *Above: Setting off at last.*

23. *Left: Hands calloused and blistered from the rowing.*

24. *Below: My parrots enjoying the adventure.*

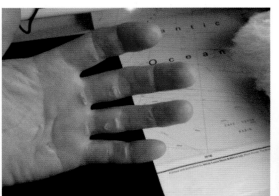

25. *Left: First thing in the morning with the sea like a millpond.*

The weekend was not, of course, just about me. Sport England and SportsAid were there to promote their organisations to the full, but my project was certainly an integral element, and rowing was very much the main theme. Visitors sweated on the rowing machines, racing against each for the best times; children coloured in sport-related pictures or exerted themselves in the junior gym. Everyone was encouraged to donate something for every mile I rowed and guess how long it would take me to cross the ocean, while the giant screen pumped out images of young people pursuing active sports, interspersed with the DVD of my boat being built. Each day *Solo* was officially unveiled as *Positive Outcomes*, and my world-record attempt to be the first Englishman to sail and row the Atlantic was announced. Relentless adrenaline-inducing activity left me drained at the end of both days, but there was general agreement it had been a successful event all round.

Amid the buzz, the noise and razzamatazz though I still felt detached from my immediate surroundings. My thoughts were often drawn to Rudyard Lake, of getting *Solo* into the water, seeing what she felt like afloat, wondering how easy she would be to row…or how hard. I kept drifting off to the prospect of that first launch, just me and my boat, with a month to get to know each other before I despatched her to foreign shores. Superficially enjoying the Trafford weekend, I just wanted it behind me, keen to get back to the real business and away from promotion activities. However, it was not quite all over. Granada TV wanted to visit the boat to do a filmed piece, and several other radio interviews with the BBC were planned, but that then was the end of immediate media commitments. I needed to spend time on the water rowing, to experience a few hundred miles of rowing, to get the muscle memory going, to evaluate an optimum pace and identify how my body and sugar levels would react to the inevitable long-term stresses.

I'd agreed with the Trafford Centre that, in accordance with their access and risk assessment procedures, I wouldn't remove the boat until the early hours of Monday morning. Phil, my buddy, had come down to help with the weekend and he agreed to wait with me, help get the boat off the stage and hooked onto the trailer. We packed up, trailered her then cleared away all the promotional materials. It had been a busy weekend and we were both watching the clock, awaiting the time when we could push her through the Trafford Centre via some especially wide delivery doors and back into the fresh air. An eerie feeling pervaded the mall as we manhandled the heavy trailer through deserted avenues of silent shops, waving to the occasional security guards wandering around; to think that over half a million people had passed through these shops over the weekend and now the retail therapy had ceased for a few short hours: a peculiar, expectant silence, watched over by sightless manikins and broken only by the panting and pushing of two shadowy, half-lit figures. Like thieves in the night we stole away, leaving behind the echoes and memories of our labours. The next time I'd reflect on the event I'd probably be exhausted, rolling with the swell and gazing at an infinite ocean. Completely alone.

CHAPTER EIGHT

Launch time at Rudyard

*Pain ripped down my whole body, stunning me with a kaleidoscope of
colours*

ON A COOL, CRISP November morning I loaded an array of
tools and various bits and bobs into the van, hooked up the boat
and was away. I'm lucky that the Rudyard reservoir is only a short
fifteen-minute drive from where I live, and as I took the road that
dropped into the valley I could see the large silver ribbon beckoning
through the trees. Clearly conditions on an inland lake weren't going
to be same as an ocean, but they would be more effective for trials
and just generally getting the feel of things. Being so close to home
I could spend as much time as possible with *Solo*, and I felt a surge
of anticipation as I parked up near the slipway. Rudyard Lake is a
long reservoir, about a couple of miles in total, nestling between
thickly wooded hillsides in the heart of the Staffordshire moorlands;
a beautiful setting not far from the main Macclesfield-to-Leek road,
and a firm favourite with walkers, cyclists, sailors and one virgin rower.
Constructed in 1797 to feed the ever-growing system of canals that
were the lifeblood of the Industrial Revolution, Rudyard became
popular once the Staffordshire Railway Company built a line along
its shore. In 1863 John Lockwood Kipling and Alice MacDonald

courted here, subsequently marrying and naming their son after the lake. The famous trapeze artist Blondin and Captain Webb of Channel fame also entertained the Victorian day-trippers, so I was conscious of the mantle of history cloaking the waters. Today those waters were tranquil and ideal for working a rhythm with the oars, but Rudyard lies within a funnel leaving it exposed to winter north-westerlies. Ferocious winds can suddenly sweep down its length, creating swirling crosswinds and challenging conditions for handling any craft

As I pulled up at the launch area I was greeted by Ray Perry, chairman of the Rudyard Lake Trust, and a couple of lads. They'd agreed to help launch the boat so I could row her round to the jetty. Ray had willingly allowed me to moor the boat for the month and had been incredibly supportive and helpful with all the arrangements. It was a tense moment as she slid gracefully from the trailer and had her first taste of floating. Feeling a little nervous and not at all like an intrepid transoceanic adventurer, I managed to manoeuvre her without too much trouble and tied her alongside the jetty. She looked a treat, sparkling in the bright water, though seemed somewhat small in the context of the lake and trees. The excitement was building at the prospect of my first row.

Autumn was easing into winter at the lake, the valley chill seeping through my bones. Shore and hillside trees were starting to drop their gold and brown coats as bare branches seemed to tear through the leafy fabric. A quiet stillness sat easily, with just an occasional jogger or passer-by exercising a dog. It was a peaceful, special place, especially out of the main tourist season, and it wasn't hard to find an affinity with nature and the beautiful, tranquil surroundings. I felt relaxed and at ease, needing to make the most of this short time and thankful that there were no crowds. Perfect. Now I could just get on with the job in hand.

I fitted the seat and sorted out the oars, rowlocks and gates (the bar across the rowlock that prevents the oar from jumping out). Shivering a little in the chill, I decided to try a quick burst up the lake to get warm and see how she handled. I undid the mooring line, then, with some difficulty, manoeuvred clear from the jetty to get a clean stroke in. A first real pull and I was away. Weird. It felt very weird. Was this really going to be my home for several months? *Solo* responded well to the effort I was putting in and we soon got up to a steady pace, about sixteen strokes a minute. The speed through the water felt clean and smooth. I seemed to be rowing quite well for a first attempt. Perhaps not effortlessly, but I could sense the muscle memory beginning to kick in, taking over and making minor subconscious adjustments to my rhythm and style. I rowed the couple of miles up to the north end of the lake and tied up against a very old and little used jetty, got out the jet boil stove and was soon sipping my first brew: my boats are always launched with a good cup of tea; far better than breaking a bottle of champagne against the hull – save that for the cruise liners. Although the bitter cold had returned now that I'd stopped the exertion of rowing, the warming tea countered its advance as I let my thoughts wander.

I was trying to make sense of my feelings, willing myself to arrange a jumble of silent coherent thoughts into comprehensible words. I sat there wanting to capture the moment in my head, but it wouldn't come. I sipped my tea and concluded that it was just one of those times when perhaps ordered, logical reasoning would trivialise the moment. I looked around at the now stirring waters, lacklustre trees, the fading colours, and tried to drink it all in, or allow it to permeate my soul so I became part of the whole. The torpid death of one season, the slow emergence of another. It wouldn't be long before I'd be experiencing these thoughts again but in a different setting. The same ache, the joy of being part of something far greater and elemental. A moment that, by definition, could never last forever. A wind came suddenly, rustled my hair and gusted across the lake, a ceaseless force, never tiring. Now there were huge dark patches on the lake as an incoming squall caused freshening conditions. I smiled out of my reverie, tipped a non-existent hat to nature and envied its freedom. Time to go. I finished my tea and readied the boat for the trip back down the lake. I still couldn't articulate my thoughts but it didn't matter. Life was good and my project was on target. Getting to the Canaries for a January start was now feasible, but it was only two months away. No peace for those who sought peace!

With the wind to my back, I pulled gently on the oars and started to build some speed, trying to find a rhythm without too much exertion. I had to be able to row all day, every day, for months on end, and as my instinct was to pull hard and fast, common sense had to overrule, otherwise I would quickly tire and become breathless. My journey would be the equivalent of a daily marathon recurring over a long period of time and I would have to hold mind and body together. Without that discipline I would fail.

That word 'fail'. Failure to complete this project would be devastating. My concerns over the last few weeks had not really been getting to the start line but failing in the row. In my mind that would class as failure. That prospect had resurfaced and doubts were building again. Trying, testing yourself and failing, then picking yourself up and carrying on, shows great strength, but in the whole of my life I'd always seen failure as a weakness I couldn't accept. There were many big unknowns in rowing the Atlantic, some out of my control but many could be planned for to a large extent. But, and it was a big but for me, it was up to me to determine success or failure, no one else. Success was reaching the other side of the ocean, so I would leave nothing to chance. I went through the things in my mind that would cause failure. Equipment? Collision? Injury? Sickness? Whale attack? Fire? Irreparable damage? Death? Ironically the latter would be the easiest, as at least I would not have to handle the failure, I could safely leave that for the 'told-you-so brigade'. Finding the rhythm in the oars, I dismissed the negativity from my mind. There wasn't going to be failure; preparation, preparation, preparation, that's what I needed.

In determined mood I arrived at the south end of the lake and moored up to the main jetty. Ray had seen me coming and was out waiting to help tether the boat. I explained how the wind was pulling her round a bit in the gusts and that she was very light without the level of gear I was expecting to take. To solve the problem Ray suggested using some of their big twenty-five-litre water bottles from the drinking machine, reckoning they would each weigh about twenty-five kilograms. Within a few minutes I had seven of them in the boat, three in the front compartment and four in the back. *Solo* settled in the water a bit lower and off I went up the lake again. She handled beautifully, and once I set into my rhythm she felt great. I turned around at the top of the lake and with darkness only a short time away headed back down to tie up at the mooring buoy where Ray would be waiting to ferry me back to the shore. It wasn't long before I was sipping tea in the comfort of his office, pleased to be out of this ever-building wintry wind, huddled round the radiator talking about how she handled and what was left to test. I really needed to carry out some roll tests to make absolutely sure the boat would right herself if rolled by storms and rogue waves. *Solo* was designed to self-right after capsizing but, as this was a prototype, I needed to test this in conditions of comparative safety while simulating the ocean environment I would be in. This would mean being locked inside the cabin. Ray said he would arrange for Matt and a few of his work colleagues from the Peak Pursuits Company to come down at the weekend and, using brute force, they would push the boat over and be on hand in case of any problems. In the warmth of Ray's office the idea didn't seem too daunting, and anyway it had to be done. Time to be on my way. I set about cleaning my gear, loaded up the van, shouted a goodbye to Ray through the window and glanced in the rear mirror as I pulled away; a schoolboy smirk beaming back. 'Smug bugger,' I thought and, with growing confidence and self-belief, swept all thoughts of failure away. It was Friday evening, my boat floated and the pubs were open. I felt another target had been achieved and everything was on track. I'd earned my pint; now, where was the nearest pub?

Next day I was back on the boat, repeating the routines of the previous day. I was learning all the time, and with the help of Len from Rudyard Rowing Club tried various rowing positions and set-ups using his experience. He gave me many simple pointers to get the most from my rowing stroke, techniques that would inevitably prove invaluable out on the big pond.

Sunday arrived and I found myself at the jetty with Matt and two of his colleagues, all kitted out in wetsuits and helmets. The intention was to tether the boat to a buoy with some clearance from the jetty, then try and do a sort of controlled roll. I wanted to do several, including one with the boat as light as possible and one with a full water ballast tank, a watertight compartment that Phil had built into the boat's design. Additionally, the cockpit had a removable plug in the floor, similar to a bath plug. In dire sea conditions, the plug could be removed to allow seawater to flood into the cockpit and, if necessary, the ballast compartment. It would be a weird feeling to pull the plug in a storm when the instinct would be to keep the water out, but a semi-flooded boat would add much needed ballast to help keep it upright. Hopefully that wasn't going to happen! After a bit of organising, I locked myself safely in the cabin and gave a 'thumbs-up' through the window to the three wetsuit-clad lads on the side of the boat. The guys started rocking the boat, gradually gaining momentum until suddenly she went over, spun right round and bobbed upright. She certainly whipped round and, to my chagrin, a few litres of water gushed in through one of the air vents that I hadn't closed properly, spraying over the electrics. Cursing myself for arrant stupidity, I mopped up the aftermath with kitchen roll, dried off the electric board and sprayed it with brake cleaner to displace any water. A salutary lesson: pay attention to detail.

I made fast the air vent and flooded the ballast tank. Ready for roll number two, I gave the thumbs-up again and braced myself in the cabin. It took a lot more effort for the lads to get the boat to capsize with the tank full but eventually they rocked her to that point of no return and she whipped round the full 360 degrees in an instant. The cabin was still a bit damp and I lost my footing during the roll and smashed my head on one of the handrail bolts that hadn't yet been covered. Pain ripped down my whole body, stunning me with a kaleidoscope of colours, leaving me momentarily disoriented. As the pain subsided I felt blood starting to run down my face. The offending ceiling bolt was coated in flesh and a few hairs and I gingerly put my hand to my head, poking my finger into the warm bolt-size hole on the top of my head. 'That bloody hurts,' I thought as I grabbed some of the wet kitchen towel and dabbed the top of my head. Of more serious concern though was my stupidity, not once but twice in just a few minutes. What if this had happened hundreds of miles out in a storm? If I'd been careless on a lake what would I be like on my own, tired and distracted after several hours or days rowing. Stupid Dave. Really, *really* stupid.

The guys helped me out of the cabin and suggested that a hospital visit was in order, but I declined: there was too much to do and I wasn't going to hang around a busy A&E unit on a Sunday afternoon waiting for a plaster. I felt we'd tested her enough so thanked Matt and his mates for their help. As they left to get changed and grab a well earned warm cup of tea, I sat dabbing the ever-increasing supply of blood, debating whether the hospital might be a good idea after all, wondering if I'd been briefly knocked out and was suffering from concussion. Obstinacy overcame commonsense as ever; sod it, I'd be all right. I moored the boat, thanked all concerned and said that I was going home to rest up and stop the bleeding. Overall I was happy that the boat had comfortably passed the rolling test, but I remained annoyed with myself. I couldn't keep making silly mistakes. My first-aid kit would be comprehensive and contain suturing materials, but I certainly didn't fancy having to use them mid-Atlantic.

I sat at home reliving my stupidity, explaining to Elaine how the boat had performed during the tests. She was pleased that it had gone well but was clearly anxious about the ease with which accidents could happen. Sitting there with blood still streaming through my matted hair was not a great way to instil confidence that all would go well. I downed a couple of painkillers but it was now complacency that was hurting the most, such simple errors of misjudgement. I'd been lucky to get away relatively lightly; anything more serious could have stopped the project before it had started. Nursing both dented pride and head, I crept up to bed, feeling lousy in body and spirit. No A&E out in the deep, I mused, just me and a first-aid box!

Chapter Nine

A broken back

Paradoxical and pained as deep conflicting thoughts filled my head

After the boat roll at Rudyard I reckoned that all was going okay, and with most of the media stuff now completed, I decided to make arrangements for transporting *Solo* to La Gomera, the island of the Canaries from where I would start my Atlantic crossing.

I booked the container with the shipping firm for nine o'clock on Monday 10th December. I now had five weeks left to continue with testing and getting as much mileage on the lake as possible. On top of this I also needed to get everything I would require stowed in the boat and prepared – everything! That one word encompassed an awful lot. It covered food, clothes, spares, navigation and communication equipment, medical kit, charts…the list went on and 'everything' didn't quite seem big enough for what it entailed. But I was confident it would all be done within the time remaining.

On top of getting the boat and the equipment ready, I still had some work to do on myself to make sure I'd be in good health, and more importantly stay that way for the duration of the crossing. I booked an appointment at the local surgery for the necessary injections and boosters, with no feeling of the apprehension I'd have felt if visiting the dentist. I don't really mind injections: ever since I saw a small child inject himself with insulin I felt I had no right ever to feel uneasy or even afraid again. For me it was a rare occasion, for that child it was a daily event.

The nurse was professional and swift and I felt little discomfort as she skilfully administered various doses from several miniature glass phials all lined up on the table. It seemed quite a cocktail so I was relieved when we were finished and I was out in the fresh air again. There's something about the smell of hospitals and surgeries that induces feelings of anxiety and panic in me: irrational, as they're places of healing, but I always associate them with death. My mother died in a hospice and perhaps that's where the association was born. As I let go of my mother's hand for the last time, I couldn't wait to escape from the place and that distinct smell. I had the same experience when my father died too, so maybe I associate the smell with death and pain rather than with caring.

Anyway, I felt glad to have got the injections out of the way and took in a few deep breaths of the rain-filled evening air, a stiff breeze cooling the ever-increasing deluge. Typical bonfire night, I thought, and the downpour showed no sign of letting up. I actually enjoyed the weather, it refreshed me as I strolled back to the car, washing away some of the stress. Some of my lists seemed to be getting shorter now that the boat was actually in the water and most of the equipment and supplies I would need were either in transit or already ordered for delivery. Yes, I was feeling good and the cleansing rain only added to the feeling of relief that things seemed to be coming together.

The only niggle was my backache. It was still giving me concern, and regular visits to the chiropractor only seemed to be resulting in temporary relief, the pain drifting back before the next visit. I'd been swimming a hundred lengths several times a week, which seemed to help, but it was nagging at me and as the weeks crept by I sensed it was getting worse. That evening I spoke to a friend who had serious back problems and he gave me his consultant's details, strongly advising me to contact him. The next day I rang my doctor and asked him to arrange a private consultation, as I knew it was the only way I could get the problem looked at quickly. Within a matter of days I had an appointment at a private hospital. It couldn't have come too soon.

I'd been pushing hard on Rudyard for over a week and was popping far too many painkillers for my liking. I was stuck between a rock and a hard place. I had to keep my fitness levels high but the effort was killing me.

The consultant was certainly thorough and the affected area was quickly located. He recommended a scan and a series of blood tests for the following day. Scans are not for the faint-hearted or the claustrophobic. I was slid face up into a long narrow tube, its circumference barely inches from my face, and told to stay perfectly still while white-coated medics performed what seemed to be a hugely complicated exercise with buttons, screens and dials. The machine rotated around me like a giant washing machine on a slow spin for thirty minutes, after which the whirring stopped and I was delivered from what I thought might be an ordeal, but was in fact quite a relaxing interlude. A further meeting was booked with the consultant for the following week and I convinced myself it was all a matter of stronger painkillers. Never was the phrase 'ignorance is bliss' going to be so prophetic!

The consultant waved me into his room and began with a trace of annoyance in his voice. 'Mr Clarke,' he flared, 'why didn't you tell me you had broken your back as a child?'

I'm not sure my brain took that statement in but shock clearly registered on my face for he quickly calmed down. I explained that I did have a serious accident as a child but it was diagnosed as a bruised spine. The conversation brought the incident vividly back into focus. I'd been climbing on the cowshed roof, part of our outbuildings at home, and jumping through a hole onto a pile of old hay bales. The barn was unused and at eleven years old it was what young lads did, despite being told numerous times not to go on the roof as it was rotten. As a worldly-wise lad I clearly knew better and off I went again and again, onto the roof, diving through the hole. Great fun! Then, one day, heading over to the hole, without warning I disappeared through a new hole I'd created. I fell heavily into the milking shippon (a local name for parlour) and onto its solid concrete floor, so winded I couldn't cry. I lay there among rotten timbers and broken slate wondering if I was dead, as I really couldn't breathe. On hearing the noise of the roof giving way, my older sister Christine rushed in and asked what I was doing. Talk about big sisters asking stupid questions! Still winded I couldn't answer her, just looked up with scared eyes, my face covered in dust and blood. I remember realising that if I could taste my blood then I wasn't dead, but perhaps I was dying. Perhaps I'd die like my favourite cowboy film stars who, when shot, would look up for sympathy and then fade away, usually in the arms of their best friend or the woman they loved. But this wasn't the movies, and my big sis just stood there looking bewildered. I drifted in and out of consciousness, glimpsing Mum and Dad anxiously looking over me. I wasn't dead then but hearing my dad ranting and repeating 'I told the bloody fool not to go on the roof' I figured if I didn't die then I was in for a real rollicking and might wish I had.

I still wasn't breathing properly so couldn't answer questions about where it hurt or tell them it hurt everywhere. Dad carried me into the house and put me on the settee. Now it was Mum's turn for a rant. 'He's got his own bloody bed in A&E he's in there that often!' It was true. I had been a frequent visitor of late, a fall from a tree saw me there with a broken arm, and just a few weeks before that I'd fallen and head-butted a trough, necessitating half a dozen stitches above my right eye. To me it was all part and parcel of life, but it didn't stop me shedding a few tears. I was glad to have my mum comforting me as only a mother can.

A couple of hours after my fall from grace and (eventually) some well-deserved sympathy, I remained lying, unable to move and still in serious pain. Mum decided to call an ambulance as it hurt too much to sit up and go to the hospital in the car. I think they now knew it was pretty serious as normally I'd have been back on the roof by then.

In hospital a lot of nurses were rushing around me and I could see the concern on my parents' faces. My breathing had improved slightly to the point where I could mutter 'ouch' when the doctor was doing his examination. X-rays didn't appear to show anything broken, though there was serious bruising and swelling on my spine where I'd hit the shippon. I overheard the doctor say that I had to be kept in hospital for a few days. I felt an overwhelming urge to weep. I didn't want to stay. I wanted to go home. Mum put her arms around me and said that big boys don't cry. I ended up staying for just under a week before I was discharged, though I'm not sure if that was because I was fully fit or that I'd been causing too much havoc in the wards with my new toy called a wheelchair. Slowly and gingerly, I walked out of hospital with Mum and Dad, the relief evident on their faces that the wheelchair remained behind. It was a fortunate escape but within two weeks I'd donned the mantle of youthful invincibility again and was back on the roof.

The consultant explained that years ago the x-ray equipment of the time was limited and could well have missed the fracture because of the localised swelling, particularly as it was impacted on top of the vertebrae. With current technology it was now easier to spot and as I looked at the scan I could see his point. He explained where the problem was and as it was quite swollen and inflamed with the recent aggravation from the rowing there was also some slight spondylosis above and below the damaged vertebrae. He suggested an operation under general anaesthetic and the injection of steroids and some local anaesthetic into the spinal facet joints. The use of x-rays would determine the position and penetration of the needle. I wouldn't be able to row for at least ten days and would require a slow recovery time over a period of two to three weeks as a minimum. Pre-consultation, I'd been rowing about two hours every morning on the rowing machine, then as much as I could get in each day in the boat at Rudyard. The news was a serious setback to my training schedule, made worse by the fact that I really didn't have a lot of choice. I decided to ask the questions I'd been trying to put off. Would the operation cure the problem and would I be able to continue with my challenge? I can still see the look on his face. The look that wondered whether he should get me certified insane while knowing I would go anyway. All he said was that rest and a slow recovery would allow the pain to be more manageable. His parting remark was short and to the point. 'You're cutting a fine line, Mr Clarke, a fine line.'

I took that to mean I'd be fine.

Sensible for once, I agreed to have the operation but only after I'd lifted *Solo* out of Rudyard, packed her with essential equipment and taken her to Southampton. The operation was scheduled for 11th December. This gave me a small window to get in as much training as I could while she was still at Rudyard: once the boat was lifted and packed up, things should get easier and it made sense to reduce the training and take some rest over the coming festive season.

I continued to spend many hours rowing up and down Rudyard. The bond I'd felt with *Solo* when she was being built was still developing and I started to feel that we were as one. We were working in tandem, as a team. It's a common occurrence with many seafarers: the boat begins to develop a personality as you grow together. I now knew she could be temperamental in gusty winds, I understood the way she moved and rocked; everything about her became 'us'. As with my previous yacht *Sharky,* I'd fallen for a mistress again, a new love outside my marriage: a platonic association for the challenge of rowing, a relationship between man and machine that had to succeed on the deep seductive ocean where it mattered.

I moored the boat up for the last time. Today I needed to lift her from the lake and get all my gear loaded for the journey to Southampton. It was Thursday 6th December, and the last few weeks since launching her had flown by. But I'd achieved what I wanted and it felt right. John and Ray from Rudyard walked over and before long we had her on the trailer and tied down ready to go home.

In Ray's office, over a brew, the three of us engaged in light banter and camaraderie, enjoying each other's company and glad to be out of the biting cold sleet on the lake, then John told me that he'd lost one of Rudyard's young swans that night to a fox. It angered him that people continued to feed the birds and entice them out of the water up to the higher bank. This made them increasingly vulnerable to predators and he pointed to a sorry scattering of white feathers and a black foot on the grass bank. We said our goodbyes and they wished me well. I thanked them both for all their generous help over the last month and, with a vigorous shaking of hands, I left the lakeside office and climbed into the van.

I looked in the rear-view mirror as I edged out of the car park, images of a similar farewell in a Devon boatyard springing to mind, but this time there was no smug grin. My face had a blank, vacant look, paradoxical and pained as deep conflicting thoughts filled my head. Rudyard was an inland puddle compared to the next place we would both be together in the water. I fought to keep my emotions intact. Many people thought I was mad, but sod 'em! Stubborn, selfish and driven maybe, but not mad. As usual, it was everyone else who was wrong.

I headed down the main road still with the realisation that in a few days I would be saying goodbye to my boat. I wouldn't be seeing her again until La Gomera, where my adventure would really begin. I felt like a pugilist in his corner awaiting the bell for the first round. A rush of adrenaline coursed through my body. All of a sudden, life felt very real. Very real indeed.

Pandemonium ensued in my office at home as stores and equipment piled up and to my relief the 'job done' ticks on my lists grew by the hour. It took most of the weekend to get the boat loaded and complete all the last-minute jobs and checks. I listed every single item that was packed in the boat in the minutest detail, leaving nothing to chance. A place for everything and everything in its place became my maxim, everything having a purpose and a place to be stowed. At last a year's preparation was finally packed away and *Solo* was sealed, ready for shipping.

In the pitch dark of one a.m. Monday morning I set out on the long journey to Southampton, intending to leave with plenty of time in hand. I'd constructed a special shipping cradle on wheels to help get the boat into the container this end and, more importantly, out at the other, where I wouldn't be around to supervise unloading. I didn't want any incidents at this late stage. The journey was exhausting, several times I felt sleep trying to take over despite several cups of strong black coffee. Eventually I pulled over and slept for an hour until my alarm jarred me back to life on the road. Gradually Southampton docks loomed ever closer and I switched off the engine with more than a little sigh. Missing a night's sleep had taken more out of me than I'd expected. I had some time in hand, so resetting my mobile phone alarm clock I lay down in the back of my campervan for another couple of hours.

The loading of the boat into the container went without a hitch.

I was a bit nervous when she was craned from the road trailer to the cradle, but the lads knew what they were doing. It was certainly a weird feeling but I also felt an overwhelming sense of relief. Getting her in the container loaded and ready was a huge tick. It was still hard to realise that in a month's time I would, hopefully, be at sea.

I returned home in the late afternoon and immediately got my stuff together for the operation the next day. This was one item on my 'things to do' list I hadn't expected and I desperately needed a big tick against it. My blood pressure rose sky-high once in hospital, being attributed to a fairly natural fear of the place and what was about to happen, but it eventually settled and the procedure was carried out successfully. I was left with six large puncture wounds, three each side of the spine just above my lower back, together with a sort of numb feeling from the affected area, but this wore off after a few days.

The last few weeks and days had flown by; a final mad sprint to the end of the beginning. Now with most things sorted it was a time to take things easy and look forward to Christmas with my family – a rare chance to put them where they truly belonged, at the centre of my life. Where had the last year gone? The decision to row, the designing and building of a boat, the publicity, fundraising, the lake trials, shipping and an operation – it had been one hell of a journey, with another looming, literally, over the horizon. For now I could relax and stash away the seafarer to become a family man again. Time for some festive landlubberly fun.

CHAPTER TEN

New Year in La Gomera

And now I was here, to one of the great oceans of the world

CHRISTMAS. A STRANGE TIME of year at best: genuine delight as the boys scrabbled to open presents and play with their toys, but there remained the subject that dare not speak its name. The dark cloud of my impending departure hovered in the air, and although we all had a great time with family and friends, whenever rowing was raised in conversation I felt I had to be dismissive and move on quickly. Christmas went and New Year was fast approaching. I was booked on the eight o'clock flight, 2nd January 2008. Only days away but time elapsed inconsistently: some hours sped by while others ticked on lethargically. I wondered whether condemned prisoners throughout history had had the same experience as they awaited the gallows. Just get on with it.

As New Year's Eve approached the tension racked up several notches and the strain on my family was all too visible. Our elder son, Bradley, had started to get quite emotional and his eyes seemed permanently full of tears, only awaiting release. Feelings of selfishness surfaced again. The row was never far from my thoughts and I was always conscious of operating on two levels, in the role of happy father and husband while thinking of the days ahead. Seeing the boys clearly upset had me wondering what would happen if I failed to return, if the ocean saw fit to claim me. Last-minute doubts and fears played their familiar tunes, together with the overwhelming urge to cancel everything and play safe. Deep fears, but still not as deep as the desire to go. I could rationalise the emotions, and convince myself they were the normal leaving pangs, but it didn't feel that way when my boys slung their arms around me and gripped me tightly.

New Year's Day was spent in a state of melancholy. The reality of leaving was now just a few hours away and my bags were packed and ready in the hall. Our family dinner was awkward, with difficult and tense undertones, though I tried my best to lighten the atmosphere. As long as we didn't think about my leaving, we were just another happy family, enjoying the moment and trying hard to put off the inevitable. As night came I said goodbye to my boys, Bradley and Joel, as I tucked them into bed, fighting back my own tears as I wiped away theirs; a horrible, horrible, gut-wrenching experience that can't really be described. Fear, love, guilt and despair tore at my conscience and the tears flowed down my cheeks as I went back downstairs. I sat on the bottom step trying to get myself together before going through to Elaine. I had to be strong for them all but was finding it very hard to keep the lid on my emotions. I caught Elaine's look as I re-entered our living room and knew she was suffering inner turmoil for us all. We just acted as normal, going through the motions and watching a few bits on television. Going to bed felt like that long walk to the gallows, an inevitability. We kissed and said our goodbyes before we both drifted off to tormented sleep: so much to say, so little to be said. I would be leaving at five o'clock the next morning.

I slept fitfully for a few hours and it was something of a relief when I got up at about three o'clock and went down to my office, sipping tea and sending out some final emails. It all felt surreal and misty as if it was all a dream. I wondered again whether I really should call the whole project off. My family was suffering and I felt as guilty as hell.

Time to leave. I could put it off no longer; didn't really, truth to tell, want to put it off. I knew I'd be okay once the leaving bit was over. I took a deep breath, drew some strength from somewhere and quietly moved into the hall to put my bags outside. Suddenly I was aware of Elaine's presence on the stairs. She was clearly upset and guilt charged through my body. I felt full of remorse, hating myself as I took her in my arms to comfort her. And then the words poured out. 'I've got a bad feeling about this,' she admitted. 'I don't want you to go.'

What could I do? I felt dreadful. Conflicting thoughts raced through my head. It was too late to turn back. Too late to explain the deep motives and need to meet this challenge. I had to prove to myself that I could successfully accomplish it, a selfish but very necessary desire. I had a sudden insight as to the irrational madness of it all. There was no logical reason to row the Atlantic, but this wasn't about sane reason. I just knew I had to do it. Was it for the freedom? A ridiculous need to prove myself? I pushed the dark thoughts away, knowing I had to be strong.

I reassured Elaine as best I could that I would be fine and eventually she returned to our bedroom. My buddy Phil pulled up outside and threw my bags in the boot for the forty-minute drive to Manchester Airport and the flight to Tenerife. I supposed this marked the start of my adventure, but I had to push hard to hold back the tears, a cocktail of continuing guilt, selfishness and fear. The drive to the airport was a solemn affair as I stared unseeing and disconsolate through the passenger window, despite Phil reassuring me constantly that everything was going to be okay; he and his wife would ensure that my family would be looked after. I just hoped he meant until I returned.

After coffee in the airport lounge and a 'take care' sort of man hug, Phil left and, finally, I was on my own. Airports are some of the loneliest places on the planet and as I sat with my bag Elaine's words came back to haunt me. She'd had a bad feeling about the trip...was this a woman's sixth sense, did she already know I wouldn't return? Or was it just her confusion in dealing with a strange situation that was incredibly difficult to have to handle? For me, buried deep in the project, I'd not had the time to let my worries fester; they just came at me on occasion, but Elaine had had to live on the perimeter, watching from the sidelines as my project steadily consumed me.

For her, my single-mindedness would have been incomprehensible and her fears of the unknown would have built up layer by layer. Just the simple question 'why does he want to do this?' must have seemed unanswerable, so hopefully it wasn't a woman's intuition that I wouldn't be coming back, perhaps it was just a culmination in face of a challenge that made no real sense. With the luxury of hindsight my blinded determination had prevented me from understanding her perspective, and it must have seemed as though I was incapable of any real feelings for my closest loved ones. It didn't make me feel any better as I heard my flight being called, but at least I thought, albeit too late, that I could rationalise her fears. Either way, the prospect of returning safe and sound was down to no one else. My life would be, literally, in my own hands.

I forced positive thoughts to the fore as I entered the plane and showed my boarding card. High emotions weren't to be forgotten or discarded, but for now I needed to focus on the future, not the past. As I jostled and mingled with my fellow-passengers, couples and families off for their New Year breaks, I noticed a few of them casually looking over at me, a single guy, and clearly wondering inquisitively why I didn't appear to fit the tourist template. I seem to be able to read other people's thoughts in these circumstances, but I didn't mind; for me the mystery was part of it. Nobody knew what lay in front of me and that's how I liked it. Perhaps they weren't being nosy; perhaps they were just people watching others as the plane prepared to taxi. Did I really look different from other tourists? I certainly didn't regard myself as one. I was embarking on a long, personal and untested journey, not a short, soon-to-be-forgotten holiday. The next few months would be life-changing in every way and I savoured the moment as I buckled into my seat.

Five hours later I released the seatbelt and it was as if I'd also been unshackled from the project thus far, released from its burden, family emotions, boat design and build, equipment, stores, sponsors, radio, TV, friends and work commitments – everything past was now in compartmentalised storage. Now was *my* time, the beginning of everything I'd dreamed, planned and worked for. I rose from my seat and left behind all that was everything. Nothing else now mattered.

Nothing except the objective of crossing the Atlantic, solo and unaided: a considered, personal, self-centred ambition. A memory popped up, unbidden, the ghost of a conversation a year ago: 'This is Dave, he's going to row the Atlantic.' Was it really a year ago that Ken Crutchlow had set in concrete a semi-formed train of thought? And now I was here, to row the Atlantic, one of the great oceans of the world. This is what I had trained and worked for during that year. Incredible. I mentally divorced myself from normality. This was it; let the adventure begin.

A short taxi ride from the airport to the town saw me boarding the ship bound for La Gomera. It was a short passage and I could see my destination slowly growing in size as we approached westward bound. The island is the second smallest of the Canaries and roughly circular in shape, but segmented like an orange by deep ravines between the volcanic mountains. It's famous for the ancient Silbo Gomero, a unique whistling language used to communicate across the inhospitable interior. As the boat approached the harbour in San Sebastian I could see the lush green canopy of the rain forest peeping out from the cloud-drenched peaks. Once docked in La Gomera I headed for town looking for accommodation. I was soon spotted by an old spindly character who asked me if I was looking for somewhere to stay. He introduced himself as Vincent, his weather-beaten face looking like the textured leather from a well-worn Chesterfield in my local shooting club. I nodded 'Sí' and was shown to a clean, basically furnished apartment at a cheap price. I paid cash and agreed a week's accommodation, reckoning that would be ample time to get the boat repacked, clear customs and set off. Much as I would have liked to get to know La Gomera, I was keen to get started as soon as possible.

My bedroom had two single beds. I designated one for sleeping and the other for laying out all my gear. I'd bought all the very expensive equipment in my hand luggage, including two satellite phones, VHF radio, iPods, EPIRBs (Emergency Position Indicating Radio Beacon), portable satellite navigation, video camera and so forth. I was now filled with excitement and after unpacking and taking a shower I went to the town square looking for a meal and a drink. I've always tried to go off the tourist track when looking for a bar. Anything with bright lights and photos of food is a definite deterrent to me. After twenty minutes of walking the back streets, I spotted a small restaurant. I entered, mentally rehearsed, then used my best Spanish accent to order a beer and enquired what the fish special was. As always, speaking a language is easier than understanding the torrent of words that are returned so I didn't fully understand what the old lady said, but she had an honest-looking face and I agreed that would be fine. The meal turned out to be a fantastic fillet of lovely white fish, prepared in an olive oil sauce with a few fries and freshly chopped side salad. The beer was followed by a few glasses of *vino blanco del a casa*, making the whole occasion utterly fantastic. I'd clearly experienced genuine Gomerian hospitality rarely found in many tourist haunts. When I asked for the bill she brought me another glass of wine and two of her special liqueurs to try. Fresh fish, delicious wine, coffee, sumptuous liqueurs and great Spanish service for less than a tenner! I'd found my local for the duration. I wandered back to my accommodation thoroughly relaxed, feeling the afterglow of the meal, the warmth of the night and the welcoming island permeating my tired bones. Tomorrow I would meet my soul mate again. My little *Solo*, doubtless frustrated within her metal casing and sensing the sea air. Soon we'd both be free from the shackles of land and organised civilisation. Freedom beckoned: alone with my boat and anticipating a great challenge. All was well. My adventure had got off to a great start.

CHAPTER ELEVEN

Final preparation

There's an old saying that a boat is never ready for the sea

THE NEXT DAY SAW me at the docks early, and there, waiting patiently, was my beloved boat. I ran my hand down the gunwales as I had done in Jamie's workshop and felt a frisson of excitement. The magic was still there, like meeting an old, trusted friend again. Had it only been a tad over three weeks since I'd sent her on her way? It felt longer. I carefully checked her out from stem to stern but there wasn't a mark on her, and thankfully the hatch seals were also intact. Inspection over, I started on one of my favourite pastimes again: making a mental list of what I now needed to do.

The first thing was popping over to see Miguel, the guy who would be putting *Solo* in the water with his giant forklift truck. He looked a solid, reliable sort, with salt-and-pepper hair and a firm handshake. He didn't speak much English but together with my broken Spanish I finally gathered that if I didn't get the boat in the water by the next afternoon it couldn't be lifted in for another four days or so. It was something to do with Epiphany Sunday and a public holiday the following day. Apparently he'd be indulging in several *'grande vinos'* and would also take the Tuesday off to nurse his hangover. We both laughed in the same language but I headed off back to the boat with my list in disarray. I had until four o'clock tomorrow afternoon to be ready for Miguel's truck. In order to avoid further delays I had to do a complete turnaround with the jobs I'd planned. The priority was to apply the anti-fouling paint, set the rudder up with the tell-tales (thin strips of material that indicate wind direction), affix the adjusting lines to be controlled from the cockpit plus a load of other tasks that needed doing on dry land. Once in the water I could concentrate on the inside jobs.

I worked like a pit pony again and slowly everything came together. The boat was taped up ready to anti-foul by lunchtime, and I managed to apply the first coat so it would be dry enough for a second coat early the next morning. The rudder and lines took little time and, all in all, I was really pleased with progress. It had been a busy time but my mind was focused on getting *Solo* fully ready for sea; any job I could get done now would make it so much easier later when I'd be concentrating on rowing, eating and survival.

I worked through until dark before going back to the apartment for a shower and change of clothes. Hunger forced itself to the fore and I began to salivate about what might be on offer at my newfound 'local'. The barely efficient shower just about washed off the day's sweat and grime. I went out onto the tiny balcony with its great view of the ocean. The sun had set, but through the fading afterglow I could still pick out the silhouette of the shore and the darkening waters. Lights were coming on all around and, despite my hunger, I took a little time out to drink in the moment and ponder my fate. I thought of the freedom to come, the inevitable highs and lows of ocean rowing, and resolved to make somehow the most of these precious times. They needed embedding in my memory forever so I could relive this opportunity – the adventure of a lifetime. Thoughts of home flooded in so I grabbed my satellite phone and tapped in the number for home. My eldest son Bradley answered and we chatted away. I promised to send him a postcard of the harbour before I left. He seemed happy enough but I sensed things had been a bit unusual. Elaine came on the line and I reassured her that everything was fine and on schedule, but she still seemed uncertain whether I'd be going or not. I couldn't work out if this was her way of dealing with the situation but the conversation felt strained, like breaking into an alien world. My eyes were on a fading Spanish evening while my head was back in England. It hit me again how difficult it would be for her to look after the family on her own while Daddy was off playing with his boat. The feelings of guilt resurfaced but I held them in check. There was too much to do and I had to be 100 per cent ready, mentally and physically. Deep down I knew Elaine and the boys would be fine, but it was hard to banish fully the thought what happens if I don't come back? I pushed it to the dark recesses; now was not the time. Trying hard not to give the impression I was having a great time, I said my goodbyes and rang off. I wondered if the guilt would go away but my stomach soon settled that question.

I'd been too busy to eat anything all day and starvation was now the overriding issue. Off I went into the night and soon found my gem of a restaurant again. I nodded respectfully to the same old lady behind the bar and sat at the same table. She came over, handing me a bottle of beer without my asking. I didn't ask what was available, just that I was hungry. '¿*Pescado y carne?*' she chirped through yellowed teeth. Fish or meat? Returning to her kitchen, she reset her headscarf, glancing in an oil-streaked strip of stainless steel to make sure it was set straight, and then looked over at me. I knew she was as curious of my business as I was of hers, she just sensed I wasn't a normal tourist. Her English was virtually non-existent and she was smart enough to realise a full conversation in Spanish would be impossible. For a split second our eyes met; not an uncomfortable or embarrassed feeling, but it felt like one of mutual respect. We were both going about our business, with the mystery of each lost in our inability to converse. I was thinking of words I would use to describe her in my voyage notes but all I could think was that she reminded me of my nana who'd passed away many years ago. She'd had a natural ability to put me at ease, and when I visited she would always ensure I left her home with a full belly. My nana always used to say I was a pleasure to cook for as I always cleared my plate. It's only now with children of my own that I understand what she meant. My fish arrived and again I marvelled at the quality and freshness of everything. I refused the liquors, wanting to keep a clear head for the morning, but she misunderstood, thinking that I hadn't liked those of the previous night. Back she came with an unlabelled bottle and insisted I have a glass: it would have been rude to decline. A delicious kind of banana liquor hit my throat and I knew I'd get another when I paid the bill. Sleep wasn't far away now, a pleasant well-earned sleep. Thanking my host, I wandered back to the apartment through the warm mellow air, fresh and fragrant from a brief shower of rain. Tomorrow would be another busy day and I needed to be up and around early, but I sauntered with a full belly, relaxed again and enjoying the freedom of my surroundings. I was beginning to relish this time alone in a strange country, feeling confident and self-assured. It still felt odd that I was here at all, still coming to terms with the notion that within a few days I'd have left.

The next day was, as I'd predicted, another long steady haul of work. Another coat of anti-fouling paint was applied and I busied myself with a hundred and one tasks. It hardly seemed as if I'd started before I heard the roar of a throaty diesel engine and there trundling up the jetty was Miguel, bang on four o'clock. He smiled, a contented and assured air about him. A man who'd lowered hundreds of different boats into the harbour and knew what he was doing. That was all very well for him but I was extremely anxious. The boat was laden with equipment and stores; if she were dropped onto the concrete jetty now…well, that would be it. We conversed as best we could and laughed about inconsequential things, but Miguel could tell my laughter was riddled with nerves. He explained that everything would be okay and he would be very slow and careful, giving me a friendly slap on my shoulder by way of assurance. We pushed the boat in place under the lifting arms, then he went back and mounted the forklift truck. I strapped *Solo* up and Miguel slowly tweaked the controls until all the weight was his, gesturing for me to slip the cradle from under the boat. I steadied her as we reversed over to the lowering point. My heart was in my mouth, hardly daring to breathe, as eventually the boat edged to the harbour wall. Miguel motioned me to get in, then moved forward over the water and very skilfully lowered her in. I released the straps and rowed over to my mooring, giving Miguel a thankful and very relieved wave. It felt weird being in the sea at last, *Solo*'s first taste of seawater: I could almost imagine her bobbing up and down thinking hmmm, I quite like this. It had been a month since we'd last been afloat and it felt good for me too. She responded well to my rowing and we soon pulled up to her new temporary abode.

I moored up next to Anthony, another independent rower. I knew him fairly well as we'd shipped our boats together in the same container and had built a good relationship over the last year, engaging in long conversations about gear and supplies. Anthony was, in effect, making the same journey as I was. There were also two other rowing boats in the harbour, a pairs boat with Matt and Alan rowing, and another pairs boat with a guy called Sam going solo; all three were going unaided. Independently we'd come to the same decision: to row unaided, though we could have chosen the prospect of a race under the auspices of a formal challenge called the Atlantic Rowing Race. It's widely regarded as one of the toughest tests of human endurance in the world, and is a biannual challenge organised by Dorset-based Woodvale Events, the company with which I'd been in early discussions all those months ago. The event was set up to allow rowers of all abilities and backgrounds to experience open ocean conditions, powered only by their own strength and determination, to overcome the difficulties of being at sea, changeable weather, isolation and physical hardship. Matt was the chap I'd met in the very beginning with Ken from the Ocean Rowing Society. He'd previously attempted an east–west Atlantic crossing in a pairs boat a decade earlier but had failed to complete it, so this was unfinished business for him and his opportunity to set things right. I'd also had several conversations with Matt in England over the past year and his advice and opinions had been invaluable as he was a very experienced ocean rower, with a passion bordering on obsession. As I set about securing my boat, Anthony helped me with the mooring lines, then we sat and chatted. Ocean rowing all of a sudden seemed a crowded affair. Four boats about to make a crossing at roughly the same time, yet how lucky we were to be in a position to do so. At that time, fewer than thirty English people had rowed any ocean solo; in fact fewer than ninety people of any nationality had ever done so in the last forty-odd years since records began. If successful, Anthony and I would both be part of a special and elite group of adventurers. For me success would mean I'd be the first person to have ever sailed and then rowed the north Atlantic trade winds route solo and unsupported. 'Unsupported' was a word both Anthony and I were proud of: we were fiercely independent in this attempt, we knew it was us alone at sea with no rescue boat or organisers to help us out. For us this was just man and boat.

I'm not being dismissive of the biannual Atlantic rowing race; I think it's a superb idea. The camaraderie of a group event must be huge fun and I'm sure participants would become great friends over time, sharing their highs and lows of a memorable experience. People you befriend in adversity and special situations like this usually become very special mates that you keep for a lifetime. For me though, being a team player is not something I'm comfortable with. I prefer the challenge of independence and relying on my own ability. Competition against myself seems to bring out the best in me and I thrive on that buzz of uncertainty, the 'will I, can I?' factor. When you pit yourself against your own abilities there is only success or failure. For me, being part of a team doesn't sit comfortably. The downside (or perhaps it's an upside) is that once a challenge is completed the need remains to find another. And here I was describing Matt as obsessive! Taking part in the Atlantic rowing race was not an option anyway, as it was not being held for another year. Just the five of us then.

There's an old saying that a boat is never ready for the sea. As the days ticked by and while the 'to do' lists grew smaller there were always jobs to be done. First, as the shore list of work began to decrease, I started to construct a new list of jobs once I'd left land. Doing jobs is always a never-ending cycle of activity, which can be good fun. I began to put the final touches to my cabin insulation, the intention being to keep the cabin cool if it was hot and keep it warm at night if it was cool. I'd also fixed foam on all offending bolts, then covered them in insulation, all firmly glued and gaffer-taped down. Pleased that it was a job well done, I wiped the sweat from my forehead, feeling for the still tender impression in my skull when it impacted with one offending bolt at Rudyard Lake. Pain is a great teacher and it was an experience that I didn't fancy repeating, especially at sea alone.

It was another job off the list and I was looking forward to moving into the boat. The cabin was almost ready to sleep in and all the lockers would be packed with gear and equipment by the next day. Once that stage was done I'd finish off repacking the other lockers and a few other bitty jobs I'd left. I also needed to make the sheepskin covers for the rowing seat, which took me almost a day of concentrated work with needle and thread. Theoretically, by using untreated sheep wool that was full of natural oils, it would keep the inevitable bum blisters at bay for longer. Never before had I put so much faith in a woolly animal.

Mentally I now felt ready, focused and keen to leave. The weekend passed easily and by Monday evening I was itching to go. I was due to leave my apartment on the Wednesday, move the rest of my gear on Tuesday, have a night on the boat while at mooring, then set off on Thursday. Lists were full of ticks and everything was on schedule.

The Spanish authorities still hadn't given me clearance to leave and I found myself yet again in the harbour office paying another 300 euros for some sort of recovery insurance. It felt like yet another Spanish backhander, the whole bureaucratic nonsense beginning to get silly. I knew though of boats that had been impounded at the harbour when owners had tried to depart without the correct paperwork. The Spanish would simply go out to sea, tow them back and impound their boats. This would be serious, as it would mean that my year's project would be over and big fines would need to be paid before any other attempts, assuming of course I could get past the Spanish paperwork or indeed afford the alleged bribes. Rumour had been circulating that an impounded boat could cost around 30,000 euros to be released. I had no choice but to smile sweetly and cough up the cash.

I checked out of my apartment and posted the keys through the letterbox as Victor had requested, then wandered over to the harbour office to find I still didn't have clearance. Frustration was building but I managed to hold it in check. Getting arsy wasn't going to help and I was mindful that my behaviour could influence the ability of other independents to settle their own departure affairs.

The officials promised that my clearance would come the next day, something they'd been saying for a week. With another weekend looming, I needed that clearance. Harbour rot was starting to set in and I was getting anxious.

Shortly before dusk on the Wednesday evening, I wandered off to the harbour wall, seeking solitude and gazing south on the heading I would hopefully be setting off on tomorrow. Restless, I clambered down the sea wall and over to a small, deserted beach.

Broad sweeping thoughts coalesced. I was lost in an unseen panoramic expanse, splintered beyond my normal comprehension, thoughts momentarily stalled by the vastness of the ocean…*my* ocean. Tomorrow I would set off, not quite into the unknown but into the unknowing. I relaxed, let my hands sink down into the dark volcanic sand, legs outstretched, savouring an inner peace. It had taken so long to get here, so busy focusing on and managing the project that, as far as I was concerned, rowing the ocean was merely the easy bit left to do. And the start was almost upon me. I stood and dusted the sand off my hands. The quiet moment had passed and I wandered back to the town. That night I needed noise and smells, hooting horns and people around me, I tasted exhaust fumes and barbecued fish in the air. Once at sea I would drift back to this moment many times when I'd start to miss human companionship and all the things I'd taken for granted. I found a busy bar and ordered a cool beer, soaking up the atmosphere yet feeling detached and away from my body. Things seemed blurred and unfocused, not through alcohol but a kind of relaxed dreamy state, anticipating what was to come, trying to absorb the moment while it lasted. Eventually I wandered back to my boat, grabbed a pencil and tried to get my feelings down, scratching at the paper as I opened my mind's thoughts and immortalised them in print. Such is the freedom of writing, that special place where writers are alone, isolated within their imagination. Trying to capture spirit and sentiment, the essence of what is seen and felt.

I scribed a few lines in my diary. The page headed as Wednesday 9th January 2008, the eve of my row – Row Eve, I joked to myself.

Not quite Christmas Eve but I felt just as excited, recalling those heady Christmases as a child when everything seemed sprinkled with magical fairy dust. I flicked through the previous pages and all the jobs I had been ticking off as I checked and rechecked everything on the boat. Already I'd been here a week. As I read more pages my eyelids grew heavy and I soon drifted off in a peaceful sleep. A last thought burning in my mind, penned centuries before by that great ancient Roman philosopher Seneca: 'It is not because things are difficult that we do not dare, it is because we do not dare that they are difficult.'

Chapter Twelve

Delays

Frustration turned to anger

I WOKE UP IN my tiny cabin and for a moment didn't register where I actually was. It was my first full night's sleep in the cabin and today I should get the official clearance, hopefully by lunchtime, with barely six hours to go.

I had a quick wash, dressed, then just sat out on the boat going through a mental checklist. Although I tried to assume a relaxed state, I could feel my heart bumping beneath my ribcage as if determined to raise my blood pressure. I probably resembled a duck looking calm on the surface yet feet paddling like mad underwater.

I calmed myself down with a brew and enjoyed watching the harbour wake up and people go about their daily business. I saw the baker's van drop off fresh pastries outside the nearby, well-patronised coffee shop. They'd be open at seven and I would be first in line for a milky cappuccino and fresh Danish pastry, or maybe a *pain au chocolat*. Maybe this morning I would take both. Maybe I would get a couple for tomorrow too, but reckoned they wouldn't be the same – although delicious they soon lost their freshness. Fresh coffee and pastries, in the morning sun, in a sleepy café looking out into the Atlantic – no wonder they tasted so good! Enjoy them, Dave, there'll be no more for a while.

Solo and I were now ready so I sauntered over, a contented man, and duly devoured two pastries and several coffees. Life was good and I wanted to savour the last few hours on shore. Time ticked slowly as I awaited the harbour office opening and the chance to get my papers stamped so I could leave. I gave them until after ten to avoid the morning rush when hopefully they'd be more patient with my slowly improving Spanish. Finally I stood up, stretched and walked nonchalantly into the harbour office and spoke to Andres, the harbour manager. Immediately I knew by the look on his face that the news was not favourable. He rambled on about still not getting clearance from *El Capitano* in Gran Canaria and that everything was out of his control. My frustration turned to anger and I vented it on Andres. I'd been chasing the documentation ever since I'd arrived in La Gomera and still everything was *mañana*, bloody *mañana*. He took it stoically but said it would now be next week before anything could be done. I stormed off and sat outside trying to gather myself and calm down. This was just stupid madness. I was physically and mentally ready to go. Everything was sorted but the journey of a lifetime had been stymied by a piece of sodding paper and inept bureaucracy. With venom still in my voice I went over to tell the guys. They stared in disbelief. Anthony was particularly concerned as he was hoping to get clearance to leave a few days after me. Alan and Matt wanted to go as soon as possible and were just as frustrated. Sam wasn't in so much of a rush to leave but was equally disconcerted. Brilliant, I thought, all our individual efforts over many months thwarted by paperwork. With dark humour I sarcastically declared that we were now all in the same boat. No one laughed at the pun.

An hour later I returned to discuss the situation with Andres. In fairness he was trying to be helpful and I realised it was beyond his control. I asked him what would happen if I set off without clearance, would I get towed back in and the boat impounded? He gave me a look full of meaning. It was possible, he said, but unlikely. I quizzed him further. It appeared that the towing boat was actually in dry dock for repair after an argument with a large rock. I nodded understanding. He was trying to tell me that if I left they wouldn't come after me. I reckoned that, once in international waters, they couldn't do a lot anyway as I was a British citizen. It sounded logical but I wondered if the sight of a Spanish gunship bearing down on me might make me think differently.

I was strongly tempted to go anyway but I had to be considerate to the other guys. I didn't want to be the instigator in wrecking everyone's projects through my own selfishness. I wondered about going that night under cover of darkness, just slip the lines and sneak out. But if I was caught, then what?

I took a decision and told the other guys. 'It's Friday tomorrow and nothing will happen over the weekend. Even if El Capitano gave me clearance on Monday it would be the next day before I could go at the earliest. I can't afford to wait.' I looked at the lads and said, 'To hell with it, I'm going tomorrow.' Matt and Alan agreed they would too. Anthony and Sam decided they'd leave over the weekend. Immediately I felt better. I'd made a decision. The die was cast for good or ill. It was now mid-afternoon and no matter what, I was going at lunchtime tomorrow. If anybody asked, I was going out for a row. I figured that if I left about noon I would have plenty of daylight to get adjusted to the journey. Hopefully nothing would happen quickly if I was spotted, especially on a Friday afternoon and the run-up to the weekend siesta. I'd continue to row through the night and then they'd have a devil of a job trying to find me by Saturday morning. It was a plan. I'd talked myself into thinking it was foolproof.

I returned to the café and ordered yet more coffee and tapas, still hungry despite the disappointment and apprehension with my illegal departure plans. I sought comfort in the many small dishes of food, knowing I'd have to ride out the frustration for another night. Tomorrow couldn't come soon enough but I had to try and relax. Through no fault of its own, La Gomera was beginning to lose its appeal. An ocean was calling my name.

I sat on the boat for the rest of the evening, messing with the spares and listlessly double-checking everything I could, no real reason for doing so but just wanting to keep busy. I desalinated some water and made sure the filters were clean and watertight. At nearly £5,000 the water-maker unit would run from battery power charged daily by solar panels. It was such an important piece of equipment, as without a daily water supply I wouldn't survive. I did have a manually operated backup but it would take about an hour to hand pump a day's supply of water. The electric one would desalinate more than enough for a day in just over half an hour and the flick of a switch. It was worth making one more check. With nothing else to do I decided on an early night so I would be fresh for the morning.

Morning soon came and I was up and around early, getting everything stowed and ready for the off. To appease my conscience, I called at the harbour office just in case, but there was no news. Fair enough: I'd appeased my conscience: I'd go at noon all the same and take my chances.

The morning drifted by and before long I saw the harbour office closing at noon. I turned to see Matt and Alan rowing out very quietly, with no waving flags or cheers, just stealthily slipping by. I gave them a broad smile and sloppy American-style salute as they headed through the harbour entrance. I double-checked everything then suddenly realised I'd forgotten to send my sons their postcards. Shaking my head at Anthony who was waiting to see me depart, I grabbed the cards from the cabin, leapt off the boat and went over to the post box. As they slipped from my hand it hit me what I was letting go. These postcards might become Joel and Bradley's treasured keepsakes from their late dad. Would they keep them in a box as I do with trinkets from my own father? How would they remember me? A stupid selfish parent or a receding memory of someone they loved? Would they rip them up in anger or hold them tightly in remembrance?

I swallowed hard, trying to push morbid thoughts away. Whatever my fate I hoped that if anything did happen, my family would try to understand that it was my own choice. If fate deemed I wasn't to return, then for me there would be no regrets about the journey, only regrets of what I was leaving behind.

I walked back to the boat where Anthony was primed ready to hand me my lines. I shook his hand and he passed them over, my final tie with land and safety. Now there was no turning back. I placed one ore in the rowlock as he pushed me out into the harbour, dropped the other oar in the water then turned the boat and pulled off the first stroke of what would be many thousands. With a casual nod, hiding an ocean of emotions, I said, 'See you on the other side of the pond, mate.'

CHAPTER THIRTEEN

Away at last

Now very much alone, it all felt rather surreal

I EASED OUT OF the harbour entrance: no one gave me a second glance. I waved to Anthony as he took a final few photographs, then began to focus on the rowing. The afternoon was fine and sunny, the harbour waters as calm as a millpond, tempting me into complacency. I wasn't fooled by this gentle send-off, however, this false ocean invitation willing me to its charms. I'd be at sea for a long time and would experience all her moods, no day being the same, each one throwing up a new challenge. Once clear of the safety of the islands, I knew I'd get anything and everything from calm conditions to sudden storms, confused waters and rolling waves. And then the return to the calm: always the strange beguiling calm.

It was an extraordinary feeling to pull away from the safety of La Gomera, quite alien and bizarre in many ways. A bit like leaving the comfort and safety of the womb that was human society. One that I took for granted: rules and procedures, systems and infrastructure that governed and underpinned much of my behaviour and experience. Leaving the harbour for a vast nothingness was a very tangible way of leaving my organised world behind. As of that moment, every day would be the same and every day would be different, ordained only by my own rules and behaviour. Interesting: already I'd begun to philosophise about my journey – perhaps I just ought to deal with the here and now, sneaking out without the Spanish navy hauling me back! I rowed due south, watching the town slowly fade and shrink in the afternoon heat. Now very much alone, it all felt rather surreal, as if I'd suddenly wake from a dream. I knew from previous sailing experiences that this transition would be one of the hardest parts of the journey, but it wasn't a negative feeling. Truth to tell I was already enjoying myself, focusing on the rowing and allowing my mind to freefall. It all felt so natural.

I paced myself at the oars, not wanting to over-tire myself. The sun was beating down, midday being the hottest part of the day, and I didn't want to start the journey of a lifetime with sunstroke. And already the rowing felt hard. Bloody hell, I thought, this is going to hurt. The next forty-eight hours would be crucial. I needed to clear La Gomera while leaving enough room between me and the island of El Hierro, nicknamed the Iron or Isla del Meridiano (Meridian Island). In the old world of discovery, when some observers still thought the world was flat, El Hierro was the most western island before venturing into what was very much the unknown. Luckily for me, I was blessed with accurate charts and a sophisticated GPS. What would Magellan or Columbus have given for this technology? El Hierro has a huge, rocky eastern shoreline traversed by the usual north-easterlies, and one I didn't want to visit either uninvited or unexpectedly. It would require careful navigation to ensure I had enough room in case strong, gusty winds picked up. If the present northeast wind swung more easterly and freshened then I might be in trouble. I was still anxious to avoid any conflict with the Spanish authorities so needed to be at least thirty miles south of El Hierro to feel safe from the grasp of petty bureaucracy and the possible impounding of my boat.

I rowed solidly, a full eight hours into the night with just the odd break for fluid and a quick navigational check. New blisters began to break with puss as white blood cells rushed to try and repair the damage, but it was futile, my hands had become soft over Christmas and the New Year. I pulled my gloves on but it didn't stop the blisters or painful stinging. This was something I was going to have to adjust to, needing to put the pain to the back of my mind. I rinsed them in the sea, giving me cooling, momentary relief and I looked forward to the day when they would eventually harden up. Pain is usually temporary but it wouldn't take much to convince me it was permanent. I needed to shift the focus so, hungry and ravaged from the exertion, I fired up the jet boil, my small portable gas stove that boils a pint of water in super quick time. I opened a shepherd's pie 'ready meal', poured in the boiling water and resealed the bag. Ten minutes later and with the accompaniment of a gentle swell I enjoyed the first delicious hot meal of my journey, occasionally wondering whether my elderly restaurant owner in La Gomera was missing me. I followed the meal with a coffee, sitting in the cockpit watching the night sky turn deep ebony black. When pitch black and a little eerie, I waited for my night vision to adjust fully, and I hoped for a few more stars to give some edge to the infinity that was total darkness.

I cleared up and stowed everything on deck for the night, went into the cabin and rolled out a light sleeping bag and lay down. Exhaustion quickly brought on sleep, but an hour or so later I woke with a start and sat bolt upright. Where was I? It took a moment to readjust. I opened the hatch and stepped outside to have a good look around. The air was cool and I reached for my jacket. To the north La Gomera was just a faint gleam of light on the horizon, civilisation drifting away. I could see El Hierro to the southwest and, while I still had plenty of sea room the island felt closer in the darkness. Its dangerous coastline was full of sharp rocks, taking no prisoners from errant sea travellers, and I remained cautious, sensing that sleep wouldn't come easy that night. Once clear of land I'd have time to catnap as necessary. For now, I'd sacrifice sleep for safety.

I sat outside for a few minutes making more coffee. For some reason I couldn't find the teabags. Why couldn't I find them? There were 600 of them somewhere in the boat, I was sure I'd packed them. Oh well, no matter for the present, coffee would do. The sea swell was beginning to increase, tossing *Solo* about quite a bit, the wind blowing quite fresh with the occasional wave and white crest – time to finish my drink and return to the security of the cabin. The evening's toiletry consisted of a liberal wipe down with baby wipes and the application of various creams and ointments. My body was going to be subjected to a fair amount of wear and tear so I needed to get into a routine of getting clean and making sure all the salt was washed off as best as I could.

Given my anxieties over El Hierro, the first night was reasonable and I slept well for a couple of hours between one and four o'clock. I had another coffee before first light and by sunup I was on the oars and rowing hard on a compass heading of 240 degrees, figuring that would give me plenty of sea room to get past the danger zone. At noon, after a hard morning's row, I stopped to get something to eat and take a positional fix. I was now some twenty miles east of the island, a good enough margin, but the wind was now coming from the east, threatening to push me onto the shoreline if I didn't make enough southing.

If I wanted to sleep that night then the rest of the day was going to be another slog. The rowing remained hard going but I'd got into a rhythm, and the wind was beginning to ease a little, helping me to maintain a steady course. By six o'clock, with darkness approaching, I was just south of the island. Celebrations consisted of making a gallon of fresh water, brewing another coffee, grabbing a light snack then deciding to row for a bit longer. No fireworks or hurrahs, just more time in the company of oars. I rowed into nightfall and kept at it for several hours, able to do so as the wind had dropped right away, the sea becoming quite treacly. I'd decided before setting off that I would row at night only if conditions were calm or *in extremis*. I couldn't push my body too hard or recovery time would be prolonged and I mightn't stay the course.

The mealtime routine was now established. I made dinner in a bag as of the previous night – similar bag, different flavour. As it was re-hydrating I used the time for my baby wipes, creams and ointments, all delicately applied to the unmentionable cracks and crevices where the sun don't shine. Somewhat perversely, I dressed for dinner, donning what few fresh clothes I had, then switching on the iPod loaded with my favourite tracks with not a hint of the absurd. If my 'me' time was going to last for several weeks then I was determined to be as liberal as I liked. Dinner to the sound of my own Queen concert seemed rather civilised, though I doubted I'd have the luxury of ideal conditions every evening. Nevertheless I was determined to stick to a routine of getting cleaned and changed before I ate. Pudding consisted of a Mars bar and a bag of chocolate raisins, of which my musical companions doubtless approved. After coffee I wrote up my daily log, mentioning that I'd seen several turtles and dolphins already. The turtles were amazing, and I reckoned they were loggerheads. They appeared to bob just under the surface, rising and falling with the swell, seemingly lacking control over their direction while giving the impression of not being that bothered, just allowing the sea currents to take them thousands of miles. These turtles would usually take advantage of the Gulf Stream, heading south on the Canary current before turning west back into the Gulf Stream to the Caribbean.

After tidying up after my meal, I relaxed in the cabin reading a Lee Childs novel, making the most of a reasonably flat sea and calm night. Suddenly loud splashing and a sort of clapping burst through my concentration. I put the book aside and clambered out of the hatch. The sea was full of mackerel-sized fish, the boat surrounded by such a huge shoal that she seemed to be floating on them. Thousands, perhaps millions, jumped out of the water all around, creating a slapping sound as they crashed back down. For several minutes I watched enthralled at the shimmering silver lightshow. Finally the shoal moved on but the sound of their applause lasted long after they were lost to view. Wow, I thought, that was better than watching TV. Show over, I made a hot chocolate and went back to my book and cabin for the remainder of the night, an uninterrupted night with just an occasional look outside for any shipping.

The days seemed to join together as one but the patterns shifted. I was using British wintertime and would stick with that all the way across. This meant that sunrise and sunset would start to get later as we progressed west. Also the twenty-four hours revolved, not around day and night, but on the noon fix that became the start and end of each day. A blueprint for life at sea was becoming established and bearable, though, as I'd expected, conditions were considerably cramped. I'd anticipated that the first week was going to be tough and it was certainly proving so, but routines helped to give structure to the time, ironic when I thought back to how glad I'd been to be leaving an organised lifestyle – there was no denying that my inner being was conditioned to schedules. My aspiration for total freedom still subject to routine, I found it tremendously amusing. Nevertheless, set tasks and time gave me a sense of order, and after the first week things became second nature, albeit harder on the boat than would have been the case on land. I discovered that I could row for about one and a half hours and would then need a short break for fluid and food. I'd quickly down a coffee, a flapjack or something, and be back at the oars within fifteen minutes. I couldn't eat much more when rowing as the physical exertion and pressure on the stomach muscles made me feel sick and wanting to throw up. So I stuck to drinks and light snacks throughout the day, then ate as much as I could at night. It was always something to look forward to during the rowing, knowing that the reward at day's end would be a nice, full belly and a few hours of deep sleep to counter the exhaustion. Exhausted sleep came easily, but in those early days would be short-lived until I acclimatised and moved further away from land and the danger of shipping lanes.

I still hadn't found my teabags and it niggled away at me. I hadn't got them listed in any of the locker contents but was certain I'd stowed them away. I just couldn't understand it: was there such a thing as a teabag fairy? Six hundred teabags shouldn't be easy to lose. Not having found them in the cabin I decided the next evening's entertainment would be hunt the teabags in the forward lockers. An air of desperation was creeping in, an obsessive desperation for a decent brew. I wouldn't claim to be addicted in the sense of a smoker or alcoholic, but dammit I'm English and a northerner. Tea is just a leaf away from religion. It's not so much a drink as a way of life. 'Sit down and have a cup of tea,' is not just a trite statement where I come from it, it's a request, even a demand, to stop what you're doing and share some time gossiping, arguing, sympathising and putting the world to rights. If folks from my neighbourhood were to hear that I didn't have, or even worse, had lost teabags I would have been frogmarched to the south of the Watford Gap and told never to return. Survival at sea or finding those wretched teabags – it was a close call in the priority stakes.

Six days at sea and I'd nearly achieved my first small goal. I'd almost lasted a week. Tomorrow I could mark a cross on the chart showing my position and revealing the measure of progress, tangible evidence of the effort exerted so far, proof that the blisters and pain had some point to them. Day six was proving tough at the oars as the wind had picked up in the night and was now gusting at about force six with a sloppy cross swell.

It was a day for waterproofs, though several waves gave me a good soaking, wheedling their way into and beyond the protective layers. It wasn't really cold but the ingress of seawater combined with the strong wind chilled me through, even with the effort of rowing. As the weather continued to blow up, several rough waves swamped *Solo* and I had my first mini-disaster. I'd left the hatch open on the rear of the cabin, only on the breather vent, so no more than half an inch, but as one of the waves engulfed us it forced several pints at great speed through the gap. Luckily (for the electrics) most of the bedding quickly soaked up the water. It meant I would sleep in a wet compartment for a while but serious damage had been avoided and another lesson learnt. I'd remembered putting the hatch in vent position just to get a bit of fresh air, but had forgotten to close it. The day didn't improve; several huge seas boiled around the boat and the horizon would often disappear for a split second in the bubbling confusion of the breakers. *Solo* was fully laden with supplies and at maximum weight, so she sat in the water heavily, though that also proved to be an advantage. Many times I was glad of the weight when we were pushed over almost to the point of no return before rolling back to an upright position. This was *Solo*'s first experience of such conditions and I was glad she was proving to be up to the battering. Night fell and still the storm showed no sign of abating, with winds gusting to gale force at times. The sea tried its best to roll us over but without success. I took refuge in the locked, damp cabin feeling my boat endlessly slammed by breakers, then shuddering as if shaking off water like a wet dog. Sleep was futile. It took forever to sort out the chaos in the cabin, with the water from the hatch making a right mess everywhere. Much of the bedding, clothing and floor was damp, and the cabin was distinctly uncomfortable. There'd be no way to dry anything until the weather and the waves calmed down. I'd just have to live with conditions as they were. I'd experienced similar conditions many times before when sailing this route, so I knew that things should be all right – they just felt and sounded worse in the confines of a small cabin. So I lay back and tried to relax as best I could. I even took out the video camera I'd brought along and did a small webcam piece. It felt most unusual talking to a camera in a mid-Atlantic storm, but I wanted to take some footage so that I could look back on it for years to come and relive the journey, enjoy it from the comfort of my armchair, hopefully with a decent bottle of wine. That thought made me smile. If I'd had any sense, I'd be in that armchair now, instead of locked up in a tiny cabin, damp and sore from a hard day at the oars.

To make matters worse I needed to go to the toilet: number two as it's known in polite company, a Scooby Doo as it's nicknamed at home. I'd been putting it off, hoping to be able to relieve myself in the morning, hopefully in calmer conditions, but, of course, the more I tried to put it off, the greater became the need to take action. My trusty bucket was in the forward storage at the other end of the boat. The wind was so fierce I knew that sitting on a bucket was never going to work. Now was the time for drastic measures and more than a little co-ordination. Just getting out of the cabin was risky as we were getting slammed hard every few seconds. Timing was everything in more ways than one. Opening the hatch door at the wrong time would be disastrous, and sitting on a yellow bucket on deck would also not be in my best interests safety-wise. One rogue wave and I'd be swept off the boat gripping a yellow bucket like grim death: which is what it would have been. The situation was both ludicrous and dangerous, oh, and rapidly approaching a climactic conclusion of the messy kind. I shall spare you the unglamorous details – suffice for you to know that I left too fine a line between wanting to go and having to go. Evidenced up in my defence was the challenge of trying to leave the cabin, cross the cockpit, navigate the wet decks,

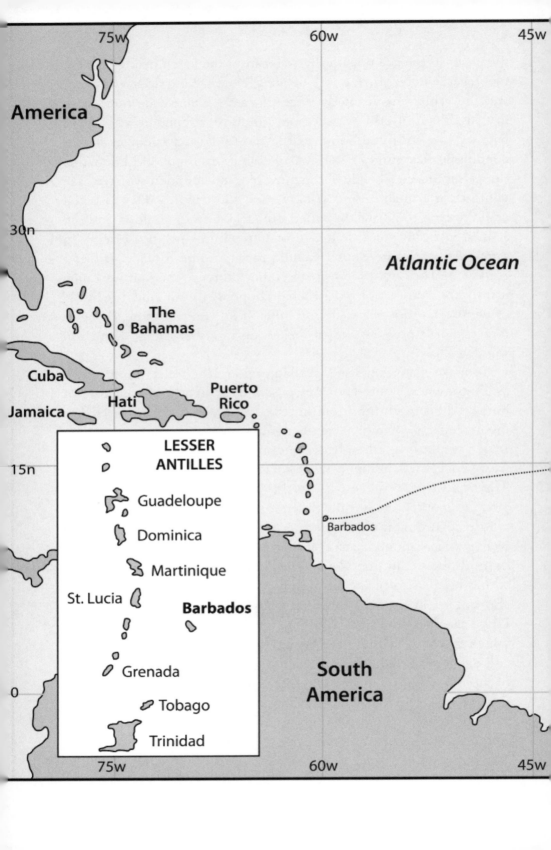

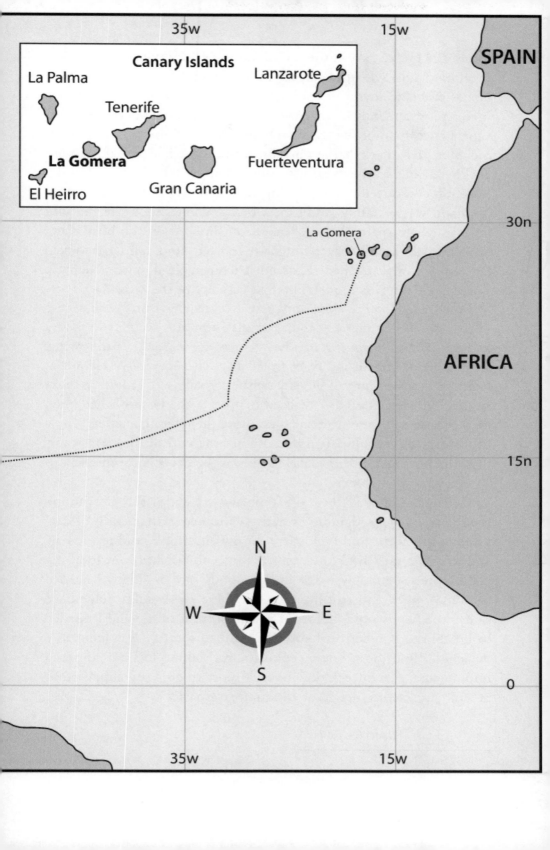

locate the bucket, avoid the incoming waves, try not to get washed overboard, and with the impact of a different diet – how shall we say? – evacuate myself. I apologised profusely to *Solo*, hoped she'd understood and hoped that the rough seas would soon clean her superstructure thoroughly, which they did. Looking back at that incident I felt that Charlie Chaplin would have been proud of me.

The next day the weather was in a more kindly mood and I looked forward to the noon fix for the end of the first week. I rowed hard and was certainly ready for a break when I took the fix with my hand-held spare GPS, the main unit housed on the boat being broken by the rough seas last night. A cracked front and what looked like ingress of water had rendered it irreparable despite it being a waterproof exterior model. The first casualty of the crossing.

I put a cross on the chart at twenty-five degrees, thirty-six minutes north, by twenty degrees and forty-five minutes west. It looked a pathetic, almost insignificant advancement for a week's hard rowing: a tiny indent and so far away from any destination. My elation at marking the position was quickly deflated. I sank into sadness, a slight depression even, though I realised that once the position had been marked that week was over and a new one then began, in effect a new beginning, but would I feel the same at the end of the next week, then the next and so on? That Friday was the day I got some serious Monday morning blues.

Deflated, I stowed the GPS unit away. I had a full afternoon's rowing in a confused, lumpy sea, the wind had swung south of east, pushing me north, and I felt sorry for myself. I took hold of the oars and forced myself back into my rhythm, initial pain from foot and hand blisters seemingly worse in this cloudy mood. I knew I needed to come out of this bad humour but there was a sulky reluctance to do so. There would be lots of weeks in front of me and I needed to be able to handle this better. The rest of the day was spent in a detached disposition, rowing robotically, thinking lots but thinking nothing at all. One week down, many more to go. I was supposed to be enjoying the challenge of a lifetime, wasn't I?

Chapter Fourteen

This weather

A boat over troubled waters

AFTER A HEARTY MEAL and some much-needed calories my mood lifted slightly, and with gradually calming seas I enjoyed relaxing in my cabin listening to a little Simon and Garfunkel, perversely messing with the lyrics as I sang: '…like a boat over troubled waters'. I was a little concerned about the depressive feeling that was washing over me, and perhaps unwisely tried to analyse why it was occurring. I'd been working towards this opportunity for more than a year, from a seed planted decades earlier: a germinated dream blossoming into reality, yet I felt sad. Why? I was now master of my own destiny with an ocean for playground and enough freedom to lose myself in. But I couldn't shake the latent sadness off. Perhaps I needed a good night's sleep.

The morning started early and after a quick breakfast of muesli and coffee I was ready for dawn to break so I could get on the oars. The sea had been gradually increasing throughout the night, nevertheless I felt my spirits lifting. What was needed was to get stuck in and do some rowing. If sleep hadn't fully cured my oppressive mood, then maybe exertion would. I rowed hard for three solid hours before taking a break. Shoving a Mars bar in my mouth I rummaged for the jet boil, turned the gas on, flicked the ignite switch and placed the stove between my bare feet. As I lifted the coffee jar from the locker the lid flew off and the contents ejected, resulting in three-quarters of a large jar of Nescafé blowing around the wet boat. The damned powder blew everywhere, swirling around the boat in a vortex, then adhering to every surface it touched, a distinctly aromatic coffee cloud that was momentarily pleasant until its sticky demise. Instinctively I wanted to blow my top but fought back the anger and tried to see the funny side, not easy with a gooey brown mess everywhere and a wasted half an hour cleaning the locker and its contents. The decks were soon washed off by the sea and eventually I managed to make some coffee, finish my Mars bar and assess the damage. I was down to one jar of coffee and with still no sight of the elusive teabags I feared I might have a major crisis on my hands. 'Mutiny no less, Captain Clarke!' I shouted out loud, releasing some inner tension. I chuckled. Either I was starting to go mad or slipping out of the disgruntled atmosphere I was orbiting in.

The wind continued to blow from the southeast and every time I stopped rowing I would begin to be blown northwards. By the end of the day there was a good force-five coming directly from the south, so much so that I needed to deploy the para sea anchor to help counter the threat of being blown back to the Canaries. It also started to rain heavily with huge thunderclouds bringing on early darkness as I fumbled with the anchor lines, a ghostly sky cloaking the remaining light.

The sea anchor is like a parachute. It has a diameter of three metres and is on a seventy-metre length of rope from a harness at the front of the boat. I had set mine with a buoy and a length of line to keep the anchor steady ten metres under the sea. I also attached to the buoy eighty metres of thinner rope to act as a tripping line. This would enable me to collapse and retrieve the chute when required. Lots of rope, all different colours, and it had to be deployed slowly from the boat in such a way that it wouldn't tangle and wouldn't get caught on the rudder.

It was a challenge, but eventually it was out and all secured. *Solo* now turned her head to the wind and rode high on the breakers as they blew up from the south – at least they wouldn't be slamming me side on. The para anchor is good to use in heavy seas, as not only does it slow the boat in drifting the wrong way, but by keeping the head to wind it is slightly safer and stands less chance of being rolled.

I switched on the spare GPS. I was still going north slightly but I reckoned in this wind, without the anchor, I'd be off back to La Gomera at about a mile an hour. Even at anchor in a rough sea my mood continued to rise. I was getting desperate for a decent brew of tea and realised I hadn't yet checked the front of the two forward lockers. These were mainly packed with emergency food rations and spares that I might not need. The extreme front of the boat was awkward to get to, as I needed to climb halfway into the forward storage compartment then access the lockers via a small diameter locker seal. I wasn't building my hopes up that the teabags were there but felt I had to look – if nothing else it would confirm they weren't onboard. Twenty minutes later I let out a whooping sound and a great cheer! I was ecstatic, I'd found the damn brew bags. For the second time that day I'd also caught myself speaking out loud. I guessed it was more down to tea deprivation than the beginnings of madness, at least I hoped so.

I celebrated with several mugs of hot sweet tea and all the biscuits I was able to dunk. Amazing how such a simple thing like a teabag could make a difference. I actually felt a bit guilty on the last of my second pack of jammy dodgers, as I'd never eaten sixteen in one sitting before, though I was keen to eat as much as I could muster to give me energy to burn the next day. I'd calculated that a daily minimum of 5,000 calories was required but assumed that might not always be possible, hence I'd bulked up before leaving home. It was inevitable that daily rowing was going to make an impact on my body fats at some stage, so all the food I took was carefully considered. Apart from high-calorie meals, I was reliant on energy drinks and chocolate bars, the latter providing about 500 calories each. Sunrise the following day was a dirty affair with sullen rain clouds all around, the only difference being their level of blackness. Clearly the weather had caught my earlier moodiness. I breakfasted on a bowl of hot porridge and sultanas, another ready meal in a bag, but after adding the hot water and with a quick stir it was ready to be eaten straightaway. It was quite delicious and I added a good tablespoon of sugar to set me up for the day. Checking the GPS brought bad news. I'd been blown back five miles towards La Gomera in the night. Sod it, I thought, but it was out of my hands. I made a brew and dismissed any dismal feelings. Going backwards now and again was all part of this challenge. I just had to keep a strong mind and deal with it head on.

It took me about thirty minutes to get the sea anchor in and stowed. I tied it all down on deck ready to deploy quickly as the wind was still in the south and I just felt it would be necessary again before nightfall. The day was tough going, the wind continuing from the south, bringing squall after squall. No sooner had one given me a soaking than another charged in, ready and poised on the horizon, lulling me into a few minutes of comfort before it began its charge and unleashed its concealed cargo of rain. Cold, biting rain.

Days ticked by and one by one the diary pages were turned over. As the miles travelled increased, so the miles to my destination decreased, a useful thought to keep in the back of my head. More was less. Week two was nearing its end and routines onboard now fitted neatly into a timetable of events that seemed to be running smoothly. The rowing remained hard with the wind rarely in the same direction from one day to the next, kicking up chaotic swells, a cauldron of confusion with *Solo* and me doing our best to travel southwest and find some stability from the trade winds. It's difficult to describe the act of rowing for long periods of time, but despite the pain from blisters (not helped by salt water) and a constantly aching body, after a while both mind and body adjusted well. Pain became the norm and was often ignored. It was the relentless regime of doing the same actions every few seconds that hit hard and dulled my mind, unless I channelled it into inner thoughts that blocked out the enduring forwards and backwards motion. Even then there was guilt if a rest break spilled over its allotted time – usually about fifteen minutes – and then my longed-for freedom became a driven treadmill. Row, break, row, break, row, break, each stint keeping me going with the thought of little rewards of tea and chocolate bars until the thought of that huge, mouth-watering feast at sundown became a reality: a real carrot at the end of the stick.

Rain squalls passed through and were followed by fine western Saharan dust, dragged airborne and carried from the desert by the wind constantly in the southeast quarter. Sand got everywhere – in my eyes, hair, cabin, in my food. Everywhere. *Solo* looked like she'd been sprinkled with a dusting of brown icing sugar by an over-zealous chef. It turned the air grey, catching dry on the taste buds, therefore providing an ideal excuse for more brews. That was fine by me. I had several days of tea-drinking to catch up on.

I decided I'd wash *Solo* off later, as even with the odd wave splashing the decks the dust lay everywhere, congregating in the corners and sticking to the cabins and hatch covers. But as the day progressed a dense cloud layer started to build on the horizon, very dark clouds: menacing. The wind too was strengthening and increasingly gusty, identified as darker patches of sea rushing towards me. Before long, spits of rain bore in and as the blackened sky drew ever closer I decided to get the jet boil on, make a meal and then hit the safety of the cabin. I reckoned I deserved an early finish and guessed I'd less than half an hour of daylight left with the oncoming storm bringing on a premature night. The minute I'd stowed the oars the skies engulfed me, moving at a pace that scorched away the final minutes of daylight, robbing the sunset of its glory. The whole scenario felt ominous, satanic even. The rain began to fall in torrents and I moved swiftly to get the boiling water into the bag of food and get myself into the safety of the cabin. Eating dinner ten minutes later I was rewarded by a theatre of thunder that cracked and rumbled so loud it shook the sea. Venomous lightning scarred the skies, determined and constant, lighting the seas and illuminating *Solo*'s topsides as the rain pelted any remaining dust to the bottom of the ocean. Although an amazing and even exciting situation, I was also nervous. I was being thrown around by an ever-increasing sea surrounded by a massive storm, but while I felt safe in it the lightning unnerved me. How would *Solo* cope with a direct lightning strike, a real and very deadly possibility? How would I? I'd seen what lightning could do to trees. And there were no trees out there, just me and the boat as the only target. Once hit there'd be no time to abandon ship, and anyway, what precisely would I abandon ship into? I'd elected in the early stages of planning not to take a life raft. The design would have required a special compartment and life rafts are heavy bulky things. *Solo* was virtually unsinkable apart from lightning and fire, so it had been a calculated risk to exclude one. I stayed as still as I could in a rocking boat, trying not to move too much in case I drew attention to myself, a pawn in God's game of thunderous chess. I consoled myself with two packets of chocolate Brazils, daring not to rattle the bags too much. Silly, I know, but it made me feel slightly better.

The storm lasted most of the night, but thankfully the thunder and lightning moved off, leaving an exhausted and gnarled sea. As the sun fought its way through to a new dawn, heavy rain still lashed down. I felt relieved. It had been a long night with little sleep, and again I'd lost ground to the north. I was keen to get on the oars because at noon that day I could mark another cross on the chart. Two full weeks at sea. I rowed with renewed energy, relieved to be away from the grip of the night. Even though the rain was heavy it felt good to be in the fresh air, visibility was poor, giving the impression that I wasn't making much ground. Nevertheless things felt good.

The noon fix was marked on the chart. In comparison to the first week it had been a poor second seven days. As the crow flies I had only gained 30 miles further south and 160 miles further west, and I couldn't help but feel a tad disappointed. I picked at the blisters on my hand and gazed forlornly at the chart. It'd been a hell of a week and the rowing had been hard – most nights I knew I would lose some of the hard-gained miles earned that day. There was no point in being maudlin, the weather had its own destiny and had become the oppressor. I felt it was testing me, testing my patience, my resolve, my ability to see this through, and my determination hardened. I went back to the oars and spent the rest of the day hard at it, the exertion felt good and I was pleased that I was beginning a new week. Maybe this one would be better?

That first day of the third week I was especially keen to finish the last rowing of the evening, not because of food, though I was weak with hunger, but because I had it in my diary to call Elaine and the boys. I'd set a day and time to call and now it had come. I removed the satellite phone from its waterproof case and set up the external aerial. The wire was fine enough to allow the hatch to be closed, and a strip of gaffer tape held the aerial in place outside despite the weather. I dialled the number from the comfort of my cabin and my son Bradley answered. We chatted about his days at school, what he'd been doing on his computer, what the weather was like and general inconsequential stuff. It seemed the family were getting into a routine without me, just as I was without them. I was bombarded with excited questions. How did it feel to row all day? Was I lonely? How long before I got back? Had I seen any sharks? Had I got any blisters? Oh yes, Bradley, yes indeed! It was good to know both boys were okay as he passed the phone to Elaine. We chatted for twenty minutes about day-to-day events, her work, how the lads were coping, how *she* was coping – all the usual domestic chitchat of a married couple. I underplayed the strength of the wind and storms, as I didn't want her to go through any unnecessary worrying – the weather was my problem and I would deal with it in my own way. Elaine knew conditions had been bad as she'd been in touch with Anna, Anthony's girlfriend, and had also been reading the blogs from the other two boats. I played it down and said things weren't that bad, the other lads weren't used to Atlantic moods as much as I was. 'Wait till we have a real blow,' I joked. Joel, my younger son, came on the phone and said, 'Hello Daddy, I miss you, goodnight.' So few words carrying huge emotions. I felt a lump in my throat and fought it back as Elaine came back to the phone to say goodnight. I switched the phone off and sat there in the silence. It felt strange to do all that talking from a tiny boat, adrift it seemed, in time and space. I played back the conversations in my mind, having so long waited for the chance to natter, then over so soon: all those feelings, then nothing. An emptiness engulfed me and I sat for a few minutes thinking of my family. Tears welled up but I fought the urge to cry. I didn't want to feel sad or sorry for myself, I wanted to feel happy. Speaking with my family had been a happy time. I snapped out of the immediate sadness and rummaged around the locker for my dinner of dehydrated meals. Same packets, same old flavours. I'd brought only five different types, shepherd's pie, chicken and noodles, spaghetti Bolognese, chilli con carne and lamb pilaff, and already they were starting to become a bit repetitive. That night I had two ready meals of shepherd's pie, fast becoming a firm favourite. I'd other meals and concoctions aside from the dehydrated ones but figured I ought to get better acquainted with my environment before I started cooking on a jet boil. Conditions also had to be a bit calmer as I didn't want burns or scalds to contend with, cooking with a jet boil between bare legs was not for the faint hearted. I also thought it would give me something to look forward to, a sort of mini-rewards-and-celebrations approach. The easier stuff to eat was going down well, though I'd slightly underestimated my need for calorific intake in the evenings. I was finding it perfectly normal to eat a 200-gram bar of chocolate then follow it with a Mars bar or two, and that was after a huge meal.

Week three continued with me drifting in and out of meditative mood, the weather still testing and changeable. Lots of squalls and lumpy seas, but I was making progress, albeit more slowly than I'd have preferred, but at least it was towards my destination. I figured the wind would eventually turn more to the north and I could then make some southing. The conditions were still difficult though and little did I realise I was building up a bank of internal frustrations that would eventually have to blow. Even rowing hard most days it was tough to make progress and at one point I strained my back a little and had to give myself a good talking to for being stupid. I had a long way to go and injury would be a disastrous end to the journey. I still needed reminders not to fight the weather.

The end of the third week coincided with the first day of February: a new month and perhaps a better weather pattern to come. The weather was becoming all-consuming, and I could now feel the build-up of tension and resentment as the days continued to frustrate. Oddly, I wasn't unhappy, just very frustrated. I'd encountered some horrible days rowing and going backwards or sideward, having to earn every mile, only to lose it at night. Some days after rowing it would feel like I'd been run over, so painkillers and anti-inflammatory tablets were now mandatory. By the end of each day I'd stink like a camel with stale sweat, my clothes constantly damp and mildewed by the salt. I had another mishap with timing my exit from the cabin and was just getting out as a wave washed. Fortunately, I took the brunt of it but sufficient found its way in. There was no damage but I cursed the sea endlessly as once things got wet with saltwater they never seemed to dry out fully, the salt seemingly holding the moisture.

I cursed the rowing too. My frustrations reached daily pinnacles, the oars jousting and jostling with each other and the sea, with me the abused referee trying to make sense of the game. Seas became akin to an uncontrollable twin-tub washer, wild and confused, wind from the southwest making any headway virtually impossible. This morning's result after a brutal and relentless four-hour stint was half a mile backwards from the day's start point. I could have wept royally, could have sat there thinking things couldn't get any worse. Then an unseen wave would slap the boat and douse me yet again. I let an odd tear of frustration go along with the dripping saltwater and just dug deeper for more resolve. I lost count of the times I had to stow the oars and put out the para anchor to help save losing further ground back to the Canaries. The only positive act possible was to fire up the jet boil for a brew. Many were the times when rowing became pointless, forward motion impossible. I sensed the conditions were gradually beating me, wearing me down, fatiguing and frustrating me. A new routine emerged. I'd finish my brew, then check the lines on the anchor straining under the pressure of the seas, wondering, ever wondering whether progress was being made.

A petrel darted around *Solo*, seemingly appearing from nowhere. A black-and-white elegance on wings, with full acrobatic skills on display, as it danced and swooped over the waves. I feel an affinity to ocean birds and love it when they visit, another freestyle wanderer in this vastness of blue and grey. This one came when I was in dire need of a moral pick-me-up, and it made me feel not so alone. It brought the promise of fleeting companionship, another being having to tackle the harsh environment and grizzly conditions. I exchanged my cursing and took comfort from nature, a smile etched across my face. Remarkable that a solitary bird could make my spirits soar. I laughed at myself and the adversity of the situation I found myself in. Here by choice and now no choice.

The petrel twirled and dazzled briefly before heading off on its lonely journey. I watched it disappear to a tiny speck, then, strangely happy and wistful, I retired to the sanctuary of my cabin.

CHAPTER FIFTEEN

Happy sadness

If loving hearts were never lonely then all they wish might always be

THERE WAS NO POINT in rowing against a strong headwind so I made the most of my free time. After a deep afternoon nap I took to cleaning the cabin, then, though still cold and rainy, I stripped off and went out on deck. The seas were pretty big but *Solo* was riding steady on the para anchor and coping admirably with the swell. Not wanting to hang around too long, I quickly lathered myself all over with shower gel then rinsed off with half a gallon of fresh water. It felt great. Freezing cold, but great. Masochism is an interesting sideline to ocean voyages. I fired up the jet boil and luxuriated in a hot shave, an interesting exercise in concentration, trying to grip a small mirror between my legs, holding onto the boat with one hand while hacking at a week's whiskery growth with the other. Diving back into the cabin to dry off I found some clean shorts and tee shirt and, to hell with it, added a splash of aftershave. The sweet smell of personal cleanliness made me realise just how bad my body odour had become – earlier references to smelling like a camel might not have been fair on the camel. Feeling like a proper little housemaid, I lay a clean, dry sheet over the sleeping bag and changed the pillowcase. Such simple acts but I in my little haven looked and smelled great. It all added to my contentment.

Now fully into busy mode I carried out maintenance on the water maker, cleaning all the filters and generally giving the unit a check over. A small leak had developed in the main filter housing seal but using special grease to refit it seemed to make things worse. It only leaked when I made water and a small sponge helped dry the compartment, so it wasn't yet a serious problem, but it needed keeping an eye on. It could be disastrous if the unit were to fail. It was at this point that I realised that handling grease and undertaking mechanical maintenance in a rolling boat *after* a shower and putting on clean clothes was not exceptionally well planned, but hey, I was happy. In that spirit of satisfaction, I did a full check on my stores, noting how much food was left, its condition and how much had been consumed. The last of the fresh fruit, the final few oranges, had mildew on them so needed eating immediately, giving the cabin a lovely citrus smell, so much more natural than with aerosol spray. My nose hinted at deprivation. Where was the crispy fried bacon, the sizzling steak and onions, vinegar on hot fish and chips, freshly baked crusty bread and warm sugared doughnuts? Dangerous thoughts led me to crave for something a little bit special for my evening meal.

I rummaged around the food locker and pulled out a pre-cooked long-life tuna steak sealed in a bag and smothered in a ginger and chilli marinade. Grabbing some pre-cooked rice I dropped both bags in hot water to warm them through. They were absolutely scrumptious and a delicious change from the packet food that was my staple diet. The meaty tuna had a great texture and it was hard to resist warming another. So I did, savouring every morsel before checking to see how many were left. I counted seven. It somehow seemed bad manners to leave an odd number so it took no persuasion at all to grab a third helping and finish off the rice. This was real freedom, I mused: no one to point the finger of gluttony and a devil-may-care attitude about my food stocks. This was the life!

Serenely replete, I went on deck for a look-see, the headwind still prevalent. *Solo* was handling the sea anchor well so I enjoyed the time on deck watching the daylight leave the sky. I lit the jet boil and made a coffee, very careful not to make the same error as previously. A large fishy burp confirmed that I'd eaten too much and I suspected that oncoming indigestion was going to be a suitable and deserved penance for my greed.

The gas just managed to boil the water before petering out, so a new canister needed to be fitted. The old gas unit was disposed of over the side. I hated polluting the ocean but spent canisters contain gas residue, a potential fire or explosive hazard in a cramped boat. The only safe option was to dump them, making sure they would sink to the bottom by piercing a hole in them with a sharp deck knife. Perhaps I'd given some proud hermit crabs a luxury new home. It helped assuage the guilt of dumping them over the side, though there wouldn't be many as the gas was lasting well. No other rubbish was dumped at sea. It all went into plastic bags and stored in the forward hold until I reached land. There was quite a bit of plastic, as most things I had double-wrapped in small plastic bags, but it was important to retain it all. World pollution of our oceans is on the increase, and while I supposed I would make little impact in the great scheme of things, nevertheless it was important to stick to my principles. The oceans are often described as the lifeblood of the planet, and we must preserve them for future generations, including my own sons.

I made a final brew in the remaining embers of the evening before clambering into the cabin to avoid the increasing sea spray. I'd agreed a time and date to give my fellow-rower Anthony a call on the sat phone, so approaching the allotted time I set up the phone as before and dialled the number. Anthony answered and we chatted away, enjoying a good moan about the weather and conditions. It felt good to offload onto someone who was in the same boat, so to speak, and it did us both good. All four boats that had set off from La Gomera were now well scattered across the ocean, and far enough apart to have slightly differing weather conditions: specks on the ocean fanned out over hundreds of miles, insignificant to all but ourselves, our families and friends.

Week three had passed and February continued with changeable weather systems, no day the same, squally one minute, sunny the next. Miles earned. Miles lost. Rewarded. Punished. Wet. Dry. Frustrated.

Happy. Tired. Always tired. The only constant was changeable weather, and I longed for some dependable trade winds and dry decks. I was settled though. Soldiering on with whatever the elements threw at me, and the ever-present hardship, seemed to bring me closer to nature. I was starting to feel an affinity with it. I could feel the wind's presence, slight differences in force, backing or veering, sensing the coolness as rain dropped close by. I was in tune with my environment – this was what I had dreamt of for so long, a part of nature, waltzing across the ocean together. And that included the rain. I stopped treating it as an unwelcome enemy: yes, it was sometimes uncomfortable and cold, but I now looked upon it as a visitor, a guest dropping in for (hopefully) a short stay. Again I embraced its different moods, light spits mixing with the sea spray or heavy downpours that would totally wipe out all visibility, losing all perspective of distance and making the ocean feel immeasurable, endless without horizon, yet often leaving a calling card rainbow after the visit. Rainbows at sea were sensational, arching across the ocean like a ribbon holding sea and sky together, while my senses were on wide-angle alert to soak it all in. Light refracted and reflected through droplets of moisture, sun and water, the gift of life showing off through a parade of sevenfold colour. Not only was I attuning with the natural world, I was becoming part of it. I was rediscovering my understanding of freedom.

I slept well for a few hours – it was a good sleep, slumber deep and relaxed. At about three in the morning I finally opened an eye to glance at the compass. The wind must have died away as I slept, for there was little movement. It took me a few seconds to work it out, but by the way *Solo* was pulling at the para anchor I reckoned we would drift westwards if I hauled it in. It was always worth getting an extra mile in the right direction, especially if a free drift mile. I strapped on my head torch, fastened up my jacket, and twenty minutes later I had the anchor and almost 500 feet of combined ropes in the boat, all tied up. I left the lot on deck, instantly accessible in case conditions became changeable again, just hoping I'd be able to get a good row session at first light. I checked the GPS and we were indeed drifting westwards at about half a knot per hour. I made a brew and sat on deck, stargazing and enjoying the free time before sunrise. There was something very special about waiting for the sun to arrive. Most days now I would be waiting as the first streaks of dawn hit the eastern horizon, my cue to start work at the oars. Every twenty-four hours I marvelled at a new, unique sunrise. Always the same, always different, colours and conditions the ingredients of variation – yet infinitesimally just a few minutes later each day as I continued to claw ever westwards. Most nights I would be up for quite a few hours at any time of the night having a brew and just relaxing, maybe sitting out under the portrait of stars such as now, relishing that feeling of contentment as new light punched through, allowing the stars to sleep.

While on deck I'd been looking at my rowing position and wondering whether to change the set-up slightly. I decided to row more overhand, risking the possibility of crushed thumbs being trapped between the oars, but rewarded with more pulling power for the effort. I'd experimented in trials at Rudyard Lake, and with so many more miles to go and a burning desire to achieve more daily distance, my thumbs were offered up for sacrifice. I just hoped they'd be okay. It felt a bit strange with full overhand rowing, but once into a rhythm it felt fine, and if anything more comfortable than previously. I could also feel myself becoming stronger. I'd usually pull for one and a half to two hours, break for a quarter of an hour, then, refreshed, return to the oars. Life was good and as the days leaked into mid-February I was well into the swing of my journey. Marking the fourth week's fix on the chart seemed ages ago and I was now fast approaching the end of my fifth week at sea. The days were flying by: no sooner had I started rowing at daybreak than I'd be eating my evening meal as the sun set. The weather was still my master, testing me constantly, but I'd come to terms with it more, almost revelling in the challenge and hardship that presented themselves daily. Losing miles at night remained frustrating and on the few occasions when I came up against headwinds, I'd trouble making twelve miles a day. A full day's rowing at one nautical mile per hour was challenging. Increasingly my mind drifted off to other quarters. I daydreamed of being beamed up and transported back into reality. I fantasised about food, running water, hot baths, friends, family, and laughter. These thoughts made me happy and I listed in my mind what I might do first. A hot bath then steak and chips won the daydream, but alas reality was a brew and two Mars bars. Not quite the same, but it energised me enough for the next two-hour stint. I'd kept a slab of Jamaican ginger cake sparingly sidelined for breaks, so it made a welcome change from chocolate.

Sea life had been building up over the last few weeks, and it'd been keeping me amused. About a dozen or so little stripy perch-like fish had been living under the boat for a while. I'd been feeding them crumbs from my biscuits, and on calm days they would take small titbits from my fingers. One evening I was rinsing out the dinner pan and washed the rice residue overboard. It caused a heck of a frenzy, with some fish swimming right into the pan to get at the rice, not bothering about me in the slightest, just happy for a free meal and the security of my boat.

I'd also got a few large dorados following *Solo*. Dorados are also known as mahi-mahi, lampuga or dolphinfish, and are large surface-dwelling carnivorous animals with gold, green and blue bodies that glisten in the light. Mahi-mahi incidentally is an Hawaiian word meaning *very strong*. They didn't seem to bother with the stripies, preferring to head off to find the flying fish that they seem constantly to feed on. My own private dorado shoal seemed to be building and I was sure I could recognise them individually, to the point where I actually gave them names, Goldie, Stumpy, Ugly and Leroy. I know, who the heck calls a fish Leroy! This was amusing and disconcerting. Another sign of madness or just a longing for some company, any company? I would feed the dorados every morning with the flying fish that had landed on deck overnight, stunning themselves in the process. These fish, as with the birds, gave me much pleasure. There we were, a little, isolated, floating oasis of nature: it made me feel I was increasingly blending in, not so much the intruder but the guest, slowly but surely being accepted. I was offering safety through my boat and the odd free meal from my scraps. Nature as always was making use of what she had and I was relishing these new forms of kinship with the living world.

After five weeks I was adjusting to the journey well, still with much of the time lost in my own thoughts and daydreams, rowing away with

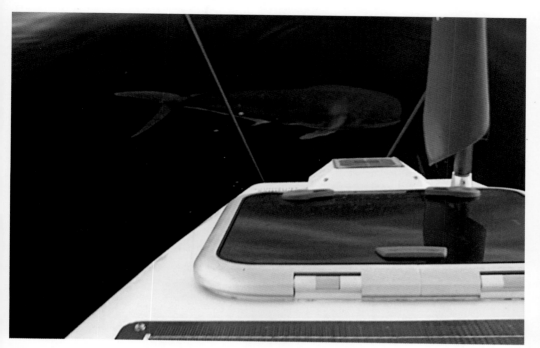

26. Above: Dorado at the stern of the boat.

27. Left: Jet boil firmly between my feet.

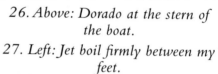

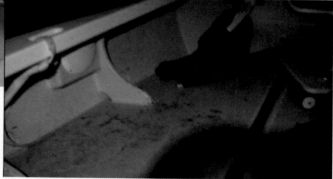

28. Above: The bloodied decks after the Dorado had jumped aboard in the night.

29. Left: Having a brew with Pip my mug.

30. *Above: Some of the various sizes of flying fish, some so small they would fit on your finger nail.*

31. *Right: Final moments for the Dorado as the Blue Marlin swallows it head first.*

32. *Below: Having a rest from rowing on a challenging but enjoyable day.*

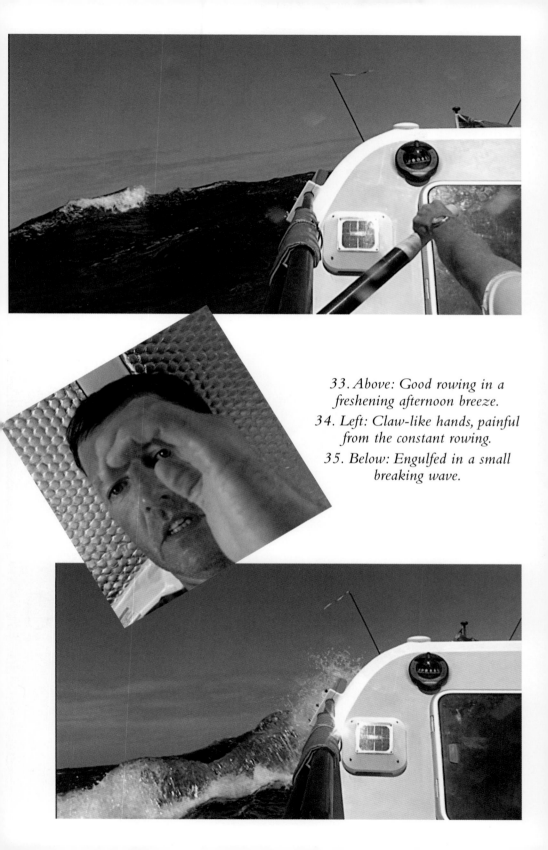

33. Above: Good rowing in a freshening afternoon breeze.

34. Left: Claw-like hands, painful from the constant rowing.

35. Below: Engulfed in a small breaking wave.

36. Above: Enjoying surfing down some challenging seas (or going slightly mad!).

37. Left: About to be doused by a wall of water.

38. Below: Breaks just short of Solo so missed the brunt of it.

39. Above left: The bird sat just inches above my head as I was trying to sleep.
40. Above right: A large wave passes through.

41. Above: Luckily we took this one on the bow or it would have rolled us had we been side on.
42. Below: It passes through with a tremendous roar.

43. Above: Wind was so fierce in the squall that it shredded the end of the flag.

44. Right: Pensive look as I realize I only have days left to go.

45. Below: Just getting ready to get out of the cabin for another session on the oars, with a big sea running, timing was everything!

46. *Above: Container ship pass-
ing by in the distance.*
47. *Right: In my waterproofs.*
48. *Below: Sunset.*

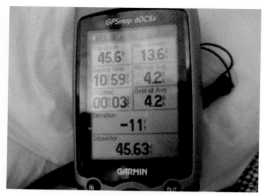

49. The last 11 hours rowing and an amazing 45.6 miles rowed, I could taste the beer!

50. Solo's resting place in Port St Charles, Barbados.

51. Solo on my driveway for the last night, the following morning her new owners were due to tow her away.

the ever-changing views, cinematic horizons never the same, never different, but always easy to lose myself in. Routines were good too. I was eating well, sleeping well and relishing the freedom of being master of my own destiny. To paraphrase U2, I'd found what I was looking for. Occasionally the weather would frustrate and it would have been easy to slip into a state of feeling sorry for myself, but I turned it away. There was much to feel happy about, so I would banish the negative thoughts. The only feeling I couldn't quite control was the ever-present guilt about leaving my family for such a long time. And not just the leaving of my family, but as Elaine had said, it's okay for you out there rowing all day. She'd never know if I'd been eaten by a shark, washed off the boat or been sunk. She had the constant worry of wondering how I was. I was the only one who knew I was okay.

And, for probably obvious reasons, on the morning of Valentine's Day my guilt trip loomed large. That night I was going to call Elaine, the first time for quite a while. As it was only four o'clock in the morning I still had the full day to anticipate the call. I wanted to tell her that I loved her and that I was sorry for putting her through all the stress of the project – perhaps that would ease the guilt. I flicked on the cabin light and put the details in the log:

Time, 0400 hours. Wind, NNE1. Heading, 240 degrees compass. Comment, light rain.

I then wrote a comment for Valentine's Day. 'If loving hearts were never lonely then all they wish might always be.' It suited my mood.

I grabbed my waterproofs and went on deck to fire up the jet boil, made a quick brew and clambered back into the cabin. It had been a peaceful night with little wind, and the light rain seemed to calm everything down, dampening the conditions. The tea was hot, sweet and a fitting remedy for my pensive mood. I picked up the log and continued to scribble some words. I wanted to capture my feelings and felt it might add some relief to the remorse I was harbouring.

No human companionship, the individual smells, the eye

contact, the whole herding and flocking instinct of man. Normality of everyday life that we are delivered and exist in – taken away. The final waves from the shoreline and then the solitude as the first night ebbs and the doubts follow the shadows as final light fades into loneliness.

Perhaps it made little sense to others, but it helped me and I played around with other words, hoping one day to look back and read my log and capture the experience, to relive it in the comfort of what passes for the real world.

The day ticked through with relative ease, as I was lost in my thoughts one minute, dreaming of my break the next. The miles were slow as the wind swung westerly, but it was light enough that I made steady progress. I was keeping a steady course, each mile gained was one less to row, and they all added up.

I was keen for the day to be over, as I desperately wanted to speak to Elaine and the boys. I rowed right up to the moment to call and hastily set up the satellite phone and made the connection. Immediately I sensed that Elaine was having a testing time, coping with everyday stresses – being, in effect, a single mum refereeing two feisty boys. I think they were missing their dad too. The pain was unbearable at the leaving of Elaine and the boys for so long. I apologised yet again for what I had put them through but Elaine said, 'Well you're there now, so just hurry up and come home soon. Stay safe, and keep rowing as hard as you can.' Temporarily it helped to alleviate my burden, but as the call ended my emotions failed me.

I packed the satellite phone away and pulled out the folder my family had done for me before I left and looked at the pictures.

A lifetime of treasured images shocked me back into the present, to that one special moment. I cried freely, the unbidden tears of a young child, unfettered and unembarrassed. Heart-racking tears that just kept coming, rolling endlessly down wet cheeks. Alone, lonely, sobbing for me, for Elaine, for my boys. Sitting in my cabin entombed and emotionally lost. Head in my hands, mind in disjointed turmoil. Finally I could cry no more, ducts dry and exhausted. A final deep sigh produced a welcome clean release to my pent-up anxieties and frustrations. I packed Bradley's and Joel's pictures and drawings away, neatly folded Elaine's goodbye letter and placed them back in their waterproof folder, too painful to keep out, too painful to put away. Happy sadness. These emotions had been building for a long while and the mementoes had become the catalytic trigger. A watershed had been breached, that haunting stage was now over. Elaine had somehow lifted that burden and just wanted me home and safe.

The call home and its impact had left me drained but relieved. The rest of the voyage certainly wasn't going to get any easier, physically or mentally. The weather had tested me, the guilt had tortured me, but my mind now felt cleansed, stronger and able to carry me forward. Big boys don't cry, I grinned.

CHAPTER SIXTEEN

Whale attack

I remained deathly quiet, hands shaking with fear and adrenaline

THAT NIGHT I SLEPT soundly for five solid hours, waking with a renewed punch of energy, released from all burdens, lifted to continue with the journey, my emotions on another level and with a sense of freedom I didn't believe was possible. It wasn't just the expanse of exhilarating space around me but an exorcising of my guilt: whatever had occurred with my emotions yesterday had worked and here I was uninhibited, bohemian, enjoying life.

The days of February were ever decreasing as were the miles to my destination. The journey wasn't going as fast as expected but I couldn't fight the weather and any opposing currents – I just had to do the best I could in face of whatever I was confronted with.

I was rowing into week six and already looking forward to putting another cross on the chart, to add to the simple dot-to-dot chain haphazardly lurching as it stretched out into the Atlantic. Although the process was still tough in the changing and changeable conditions, the further I moved southwest away from the Canaries, the better and more settled the weather was becoming.

I had plenty of food, admittedly some of the favourites had been dwindling too quickly, but something else from the lockers soon replaced them. I missed the jammy dodgers, gone the way of most of my large bars of chocolate, but I'd quickly switched my allegiance to the digestives and Snicker bars that I'd now begun to crave. My stored body fat had been burnt away and I started to feel bones I hadn't felt since finding a liking for real ale in my skinny mid-twenties.

One mid-afternoon, rowing on calm seas with sunny skies, I reached into the cabin to change the tracks on the iPod, when all of a sudden something slammed the boat hard, then again. Thud. The boat lifted and slewed around, shaking with a slight vibration like a freshly struck drum. I was stunned. Had I hit a rock and run aground? A ridiculous but instinctive thought for a nautical person. Common sense smartly nudged through to reality. The ocean is deep, thousands upon thousands of metres of sea, and that thought alone unnerved me – was it really that deep? Yes, it was! Next minute there was a huge disturbance of water at the side of the boat. Instinctively I closed all the vents, grabbed the video camera and quickly battened everything down. Was it a whale attack? I'd read stories of whales attacking boats and sinking them with just a flick of their tail. Was this what was happening to me now? Was our fate to be smashed up by a lone sea-going wanderer? My semi-resident dorados were scuttling frantically around the boat, jumpy, nervous and clearly concerned. Selfishly I hoped whatever it was preferred an evening meal of fish and not *Solo* or me. A whoosh of water and one dorado flew out of the water, as if being chased. I sat there quietly with the camera, heart pounding, hands shaking. I closed the main hatch and perched on the rowing seat, double-checking my harness – if I was going to get rolled and smashed up I reckoned it was better to be outside. The intruder had to be something big to want to eat a dorado – they were anything between one and two metres long, and quite a mouthful. I remained deathly quiet, just the thudding of my heart breaking the silence, disturbing this absolute quietness, hands shaking with fear and adrenaline. I steadied my camcorder, hand like a marksman with his pistol. I was thinking all sorts of unimaginable scenarios when suddenly the ocean bubbled with a ferocious swirl of turbulence next to the boat. I braced myself, camera ready, as I filmed a huge shadow of greyness moving under the hull, perhaps ten metres below.

It was clearly some form of dorado-eating creature, and certainly bigger than *Solo*, a shark perhaps? Selfishly I hoped it had fed well, but continued to sit there in silence for a few minutes, not really sure what to do, wondering if it would return. How quickly nature's food chain changed: the predator now the victim, the hunter now the hunted, dorados no longer a threat to the flying fish as their own priorities changed. After a further ten minutes or so, with no activity, I put the camera away and continued with the rowing, leaving the iPod off, fearing any noise might attract whatever it was to return. For the next two hours I rowed hard, then, checking my position, realised I'd cleared seven miles – it must have been the fear then. As a celebration of my survival or perhaps just an excuse to calm my frayed nerves, I opted for a brew and a snack before the final evening row.

In a way I figured that had it been a shark it was better than a whale, as sharks don't often attack boats. The words 'don't often' were okay with me, though 'never' would have been preferable. The trouble was, I needed to go into the water and spend an hour or two cleaning the hull. I'd leave it a couple of days, I thought. Like millions of people, I'd seen *Jaws* years ago, and its signature tune was firmly embedded in my mind…der dum, der dum, der dum!

The last shift on the oars continued on a calm sea and, with only a few snatches of cloud around and clear air, I knew the sunset would be yet another masterpiece. Most evenings an artist's palette of twisted orange and yellows would sink below an ocean of green and blue, the colours adopting different shades as they bounced off clouds: nature's symphony of colours, swirling and mixing in boundless freedom. The spectacle was always short-lived, maybe a minute or two at best, but always eagerly awaited. I would crane my neck, and even sometimes stop rowing to absorb the offering. I loved it, not just for the sunset, but the knowledge that as soon as the sun dipped below the horizon then that was the end of the rowing and I could get some food on and get myself cleaned up. The daily moment signalled that it was now *my* time and I could rest and eat until I could eat no more. A time when I could relax and lose myself in a book in the relative comfort of my cabin, total escapism for a few hours.

The morning arrived all too early, but I was rewarded with a flat calm ocean, so still it appeared glass-like as my reflection mirrored back. I sat outside making a brew as the dorados circled the boat, looking calm again after the previous evening's attack. I filmed them for a few minutes as the sun peeped over the horizon, absorbing the quiet solitude – mornings as calm as this were truly rare and spectacular, and just sipping hot tea was totally relaxing. Moments like these were precious and I wanted to retain the image and imprint it on my subconscious forever. It was a morning that demanded attention and I was happy to submerge and indulge myself in its sheer beauty.

I enjoyed it for as long as my conscience allowed. Eventually I chided myself: come on, Dave, no rest till you get to the other side of this big pond. Motivation for the start of the day was frequently hard as my body would stiffen overnight and needed a stint at the oars in order to lubricate all the joints and stretch the muscles. I was pleased with the way I'd been looking after myself and how I was handling the punishment. A few days earlier I'd experienced a sharp pain in my left buttock, which felt more like bone than muscle. The temptation was to roll over to my right when rowing, but I knew that would just store up extra problems, but boy did it hurt. I decided to take antibiotics together with the anti-inflammatory tablets as a precaution, hoping the condition wasn't about to get worse. I'd already had a few small boils on my face, but apart from them and the usual sore hands and feet, I was holding up well. The odd blister still developed on my hands, but only when one of the calluses dropped off.

In fact I was holding out better than *Solo*. I'd put my mask on the other day and stuck my head over the side to check the hull. She'd felt sluggish when rowing and I guessed it had to be a bit of weed growth on the hull, but I was amazed when I saw the problem. She was covered with inch-long goose barnacles that would need scraping off with my Heath Robinson scrapers, one of which was made from a plastic box lid, the other from the back of a mirror case. I was sure they'd do the job, but that wasn't really my main concern. I just didn't fancy going in the water. It wasn't so much the dorados or the shadowy creature that had taken one, though they did unnerve me a bit, it was just the thought of the huge depth of water beneath me. It was easy to feel safe in *Solo*, and here I was thinking about jumping off the side into the ocean! Yep, I was scared. I'd dived all over the world in my younger days, and thought there was nothing more unsettling and disorientating than a zero-visibility dive off a cold and blustery English coast. But here I could see for what felt like infinity through the exceptionally clear and calm water. I decided noon would be the best time to go over the side, as the sun would be at its hottest with little wind. It was also a good time to have a forced break from the oars when the sun was at its zenith. The decision also gave me the morning to man-up and get some courage. Scraping barnacles mid-Atlantic on my own was not going to be my activity of choice. Noon came too quickly and I stowed the oars. I wrote a comment in my logbook that I was going overboard to clean the bottom of the boat, hoping I wasn't writing my own obituary. It was a necessary entry in case I was eaten, washed away, drowned or suffered a heart attack. I didn't want *Solo* to be found drifting alone with people forever wondering what had happened to me. Perhaps I should write a bit more but I realised that was just a delaying tactic. Come on, Dave, what could possibly go wrong!

I put my flippers on, strapped the deck knife to my leg, put a safety line around my waist and tied the scrapers to it on a length of cord. I'd previously made a small rope ladder to act as a stirrup to aid getting back into the boat, which keeled right over as I sat on the edge. The stripy fish quickly appeared, curious as ever, while the larger dorados cautiously kept their distance. For ten long minutes I sat with my feet dangling in the water, but couldn't pluck up the courage to drop in. A mixture of disgust and self-loathing enveloped me. I shouted at myself for being a big Jessie – but it was no good, any confidence I had just drained away. Ashamed, I swung my legs back in the boat and consoled myself that I would do it tomorrow. I sat for a while letting my heart rate get back to normal, feeling very self-conscious, then decided to have another go. I removed my flippers – they were light blue and looked too fish-like – and I didn't want to be mistaken for a dorado. I repeated the procedure, legs over the side dangling in the water, then, after more a case of losing balance and at the point of no return, I was in. The coolness took my breath pleasantly and it felt refreshing to be submerged. I glanced nervously around, counting the dorados and their distance from me. There were five in total, all bigger than a metre, including the one I called Stumpy, an ugly bugger with a big bull-nosed face and menacing teeth. Together they looked like a street gang of bullies, resembling huge piranha fish and looking a whole lot more scary in the water. With obvious wariness on both sides they kept their distance, and I was thankful that they weren't too curious.

I relaxed slightly and adjusted to the new environment. The stripy fish were super-curious, and I could touch them as they came right up to the glass of my mask, cheeky little chappies for sure, but they gave me a sense that it was okay to be here. I started work on the hull and as soon as I scraped off the first few barnacles the stripies went mad, darting frenziedly, grabbing all the morsels they could. After a few minutes' work I could see a huge trail of broken barnacles and weed drifting behind me. I just hoped it wouldn't attract the wrong guests: I didn't fancy contributing to the food chain.

It took me an hour of exhausting effort to do one side. The way I'd rigged the safety line meant I had to get back in the boat to do the other side, gratefully acknowledging the rope ladder's help. A quick drink, then soon back in the water again, the starboard side taking less effort as there was a smaller infestation. It was incredible how much growth had built up in such a short time. Maybe lying alongside in the harbour had attracted the barnacles. I'd coated *Solo's* hull in a good quality anti-foul to stop this happening, so it was puzzling to discover such a huge build-up. Finally I clambered back onboard, a few barnacles missed, but I figured I'd get them in a few days. Now was the time for some refreshments. I cleaned the gear away and gave myself a rinse with a couple of litres of fresh water to clean off all the salt. Apart from the initial fear factor, I actually enjoyed the water and felt refreshed and was determined to repeat the exercise in a few days' time, to make sure I got the barnacles I'd missed. Once replenished with brew and biscuits, I set the oars up and couldn't believe how light *Solo* felt, seemingly moving through the water much easier. I rowed hard for the rest of the day, stopping only to make more fresh water and change music on the iPod. My mood was upbeat with

Solo's new pace, the weather was still calm and life felt good. Making the most of the benign weather, I'd planned to cook some pasta with porcini mushrooms (already in soak) accompanied by a tin of tuna fish and a small pack of olives. Thinking about food was a more or less permanent state. Evening meals in particular needed to include little luxuries I'd stashed away, to make the meals a tad more adventurous. The last meal of the day, with the rowing completed, was such a massive daily event that I found myself thinking about it soon after breakfast each morning, using my imagination to conjure up a rich feast of delights from what I had available. Most days I was so hungry when I'd finished the last session that I'd feel slightly faint, probably because I'd over-exerted myself. No matter, that night I chomped my way through a few pepperoni sticks to stave off the hunger pangs while the pasta boiled away. The stove was tightly gripped between my legs, something of a necessity as the pan was filled to the brim and bubbling away nicely, and I needed to concentrate to avoid accidents. With the pasta cooked and drained, I mixed in the olives, mushrooms, tuna and pasta sauce and added a quick splash of Tabasco sauce. I was salivating like crazy, dribbling with anticipation at my amazing feat of culinary skill. Finally I was rewarded and the meal tasted as good as it looked. I couldn't eat it all in the one sitting and ate the rest cold as a late supper. I was replete. No, actually, I was stuffed. I'd eaten a pan of pasta that would comfortably feed a family of four and I knew it. I did a quick stock-check to see what other delicious pasta dishes could be conjured up: even this full I was still thinking about food.

Overnight the calm conditions disappeared as the wind picked up from the north and then moved northeast. The sea soon followed, and by first light it was blowing hard, but I was pleased that I'd cleaned the hull – there'd be little chance in seas like this. It continued to blow up all day, and the rowing was quite eventful with a few breakers swamping the boat. One huge sea broke from nowhere, nearly taking me off the boat, and by day's end I was looking forward to the relative safety of the cabin. That night's serving would not be the gourmet experience of the previous evening, just a simple dehydrated meal was on the menu – it was far too rough for cooking. Throughout the hours of darkness the seas continued to build and several times *Solo* was overpowered, slewing dangerously round and off course. The way the sea was running concerned me. If another wave caught her as she slewed, then there would be a good chance we'd be rolled. The power was immense, a crazy, turbulent roller coaster out of control. The speed at which wave and wind had picked up had caused a very short sea – choppy was perhaps a mild understatement.

Several times in the night *Solo* almost went over, balancing just before the point of no return, perched high on the crest of a breaker. It was an uncomfortable night, spent tense and braced as best I could, fearing the worst yet trusting my little companion. The wind peaked some time before daybreak, and then blew itself out, allowing me to get a few hours' sleep before returning to the oars. That day was 29th February – it was a leap year – and it marked the end of my seventh week at sea. Seven weeks. It felt a long time. It *was* a long time. I'd managed to hit thirty-five degrees and twenty-three minutes west on the chart when I marked the cross for the end of that week. I studied the chart, setting myself a goal for the week to come. I wanted to break forty degrees west within the week, and as my chart was set out in five-degree blocks it seemed a reasonable goal. To get to forty degrees equated to 277 nautical miles as the crow flies, just shy of 40 miles a day west. I accepted the weather would push me north and south, even backwards at times, but I wanted that 277 miles west by the end of the week. It was a tough ask but I wanted to push harder. *Solo* was lighter now as the stores had depleted. A few days before I'd done a check, deciding to dump a lot of the powder energy drinks, though keeping the containers, amazing myself at how much it all weighed when added up. They were no great loss as they seemed to curdle in my stomach and I hadn't touched them for several weeks.

I'd also been looking at the chart to see where the destination was. When I'd made plans to crate *Solo* down to the Canaries, I'd agreed with Anthony a loose plan to ship back to the UK together. Anthony had planned to go to Antigua, as he had family meeting him on arrival. I said that I'd decide when at sea. I preferred Barbados and as I wasn't in any sort of race and wasn't planning for family and friends to come out, then I could pretty much decide, when nearer to the other side, which Caribbean island took my fancy. It was a bit like a mystery tour, but I wasn't going to think about it until I was good and ready. I didn't want to tempt fate, as so much could still go wrong, and there was still a long, long way to go. Week eight had started and I'd set a target. I wasn't going to hit it gazing at the chart. Back to it, Dave, no slacking!

CHAPTER SEVENTEEN

The pressure builds

Obsessed by the need to achieve

I WASN'T SURE THAT setting a target was necessarily a good idea, but it made the start of the week somewhat interesting. It was good to have something to aim for, and on the first day's noon fix I'd made a further thirty-four nautical miles west. Day two added a further forty-four miles west, giving me a running total, after the first couple of days, just two miles off my target. The following two days blew the target out of the water as I piled on a further fifty miles each day. Over halfway through the week and I was up sixteen miles against my expectations. It had been a satisfying few days. I actually had *Solo* surfing on some big breakers, an amazing feeling, the boat being lifted up then skimming along three or four times as fast as normal. The sensation lasted only a few seconds but it certainly livened up the rowing. The wind was pretty constant in the northeast and each night we would gain a few drift miles, a huge morale booster for the next morning.

It had been wonderful on the wildlife front too. An abundance of flying fish took flight every few seconds, exploding out of the water like firecrackers, scattering left, right and even over my head as they kept me company. Their silver bodies sparkled and glistened as the sunlight caught different angles on wings and scales. This was no entertainments show, however. The fish were flying for their lives as they were hunted by the dorados and shearwaters, the lucky ones outwitting the hunter fish with their magical gift of flight, only to fall prey to the shearwaters from the air. Each shearwater would mark out one specific dorado then glide with it as they each hunted. All the fish that took to the air were dive-bombed by birds trying to catch them mid-flight, like hawks skirmishing in a host of sparrows. Nature in the raw is so often a spectacle that makes living in harmony with it so worthwhile, living within a never-ending wildlife programme. As if the constant dorados, flying fish and birds weren't enough, there came intervals of other visitors such as shark, tuna, dolphin, triggerfish and whale, my own, exclusive marine park constantly in motion against an ever-changing backdrop of sea and sky.

That afternoon I added a new visitor to the list. I was rowing away, my mind in freefall, when something disturbed the edge of my peripheral vision to the right. Turning, I saw what could only be described as a vapour trail in the water coming torpedo-like at great speed straight for the boat. As I steadied myself for the inevitable impact, the object dipped and slewed, attacking one of the smaller dorados. I stood to get a better view, not certain whether it had got its kill or not. The fish, for now I'd seen it, circled the boat for a few seconds displaying its neon blue fins and tail. This new predator was powerful, impressive and aggressive and I knew what it was.

A magnificent female blue marlin, about three metres in length. Females can grow up to four times as big as the male, reaching weights of 4,000 pounds. Its Latin name, *Makaira nigricans,* is derived from the Greek word *machaira*, meaning a short sword or bent dagger, which accurately describes its huge spear-like bill used to stun, injure or kill at great speed. Man is one of its main predators, though huge white and mako sharks will occasionally take a marlin, assuming they can catch one!

I recalled one of my favourite books, Earnest Hemingway's *The Old Man and the Sea*, where he describes how Santiago the fisherman wrestles with an Atlantic blue marlin for over three days. Gazing at the power of the one circling my boat, it wasn't hard to imagine how much of a struggle that would have been. The way Hemingway paints Santiago's oneness with the ocean and the respect he has for the blue marlin he hunts, makes for powerful reading, a rich description, with Santiago referring to the fish as 'my brother', an admiring homage from the hunter to the hunted.

I can't help feeling that Hemingway had an affinity with the oceans and the freedom they give, the ever-changing horizons or the peace and solitude. To my mind, Hemingway lives out his own thoughts and feelings through Santiago, and a paragraph from Hemingway remains embedded in my thoughts after all these years. Having spent time at sea I now appreciate and understand it more:

> The old man could feel the morning coming and as he rowed he heard the trembling sound as flying fish left the water and the hissing that their stiff set wings made as they soared away in the darkness. He was very fond of flying fish as they were his principle friends on the ocean.

These were surely words that could only be written by someone who had experienced life on and around an ocean. His passion came not from the mere imagination of a writer's loose pen but from the heart of someone who understands the emotions involved and can express them through well-chosen words. As a young boy reading this book for the first time I had no idea that I would live to experience what it described myself.

As I'd stopped rowing, in wonder at the marlin, I decided I may as well have a brew. It really was turning into a perfect day, as I sipped freshly brewed tea and absorbed the nature around me. I was definitely in the trade winds now, hot sun, steady northeasterly breeze, gentle swells, splashes of high, wispy altostratus clouds and a few cotton-ball-sized cumulus low down. Exquisite. How privileged I felt to be here, part of the brilliant and evolving planet Earth. I smirked at my ignorance. This wasn't *our* planet. Man is just a temporary predator in nature's own food chain, albeit with a so-called higher intelligence that puts us at or near the top. We are merely spectators and recorders of events. Planet Earth will continue to evolve long after man has wiped himself out and become extinct. How arrogant of us to think we can do more than just tinker dangerously at the margins. We seem hell-bent on destroying nature, yet it is highly likely that nature will destroy us.

I think I was suffering from too much time on my hands, hence all the pondering in minute detail. I was beginning to let my thoughts and feelings run too deep, a mélange of meandering thoughts. Life on *Solo* had become compartmentalised between the physical and the metaphysical. Rowing was part mechanical, allowing free time for my mind to wander in and out of these open doors of thought. Is this what monks do, I wondered, when they retire to solitude and silence? Did they open their minds and become wholly absorbed in the meaning of life? Either way, I was rather enjoying the opportunity for positive and philosophical distractions.

Deep thinking apart, I was still rowing hard to achieve the 277-mile target that I'd set to reach forty degrees west within the week. The next couple of days put me 41 and 35 miles further westwards, so my total for the six days was 254 miles. The noon fix for the seventh day of the eighth week would hopefully see me well past the target I'd set. Although pleased about the westerly direction I was making, I was still being pushed south quite a lot by the currents, especially at night when I slept. Ironic really. In the early weeks when I'd wanted to get south I couldn't and now I didn't want south I was getting it. I eyed the Atlantic chart with a new kind of excitement and found myself talking out loud when considering where to make landfall. For the first time I allowed myself to think that my adventure was going to be successful, but quickly extinguished this growing taste of success. 'Don't temp fate yet, Dave,' I said, telling myself off. There was still a long way left to go and sod's law would doubtless have a few more surprises for me. It was too early for cockiness. I needed to keep a tight grip on the job in hand – landfall was still weeks away.

I folded the chart and put it away. I still had a second helping of pasta to eat despite devouring a lot just half an hour earlier. The need to consume as much as possible to keep energy levels up was now important, as most of my stored body fat had disappeared. I finished the pasta and made a coffee to help with digestion. Now satiated after a hard day's rowing, my eyelids were heavy, and like a recently fed baby I lost the battle to stay awake and slumbered into a deep and contented sleep.

Bang! Bang! Clatter! Slap! What the hell was going on!

The noise erupted from the deck and I bolted upright, ripped from a deep abyss of sleep. What was going on?

Slowly I shook off the fuzz of my mind and peered through the main hatch window into the blackness of the night. Thrashing about on the deck was a metre-long dorado, frantically going berserk in a bid for freedom. I shook my head, wondering if I was still dreaming, but this was no hallucination. This was forty-odd pounds of heavily muscled fish trying its best to flip itself back into the sea. What was I supposed to do?

The rowing seat was suddenly ripped from its runners and sent flying into the air. The fish then dived headfirst into the foot well as its huge tail began to bash at the main hatch. A surreal thought flashed insanely through my head – does the damn thing want to come and live with me? As it battled for breath I felt saddened to see its life ebbing away. I surely had a responsibility to try and return it to its oxygen-rich ocean, its home. Grabbing my head torch, I fastened my harness and grabbed an old towel. Fully aware of the risk of injury I pushed open the hatch and launched myself at the thrashing form. With a few swift movements using the rough grip of the towel on its slimy flesh, I wrestled it by the tail and heaved it over the side, towel and all.

Silence descended while I stood there, still not really fully awake and trying to replay what had just happened. The blood and slime all over the boat was no dream, and if I needed convincing the smell was unbelievable. *Solo* smelt like an ageing trawler, which was not pleasant. 'Could have said thanks, you bugger!' I shouted at the lapping waves.

I filmed the scene on my video camera to record the aftermath before I started the cleanup. Over an hour later the mess had disappeared, scrubbed away with oodles of washing-up liquid, tons of elbow grease and gallons of seawater. Extremely grateful for not having lost my seat, I fixed it back on the rails ready for the morning row. It was now after five in the morning and the chance of further sleep was pointless, so, brewing a coffee I sat there wide-eyed, the lingering hint of fish odour a reminder that weird things can happen at sea.

I imagined that the dorado had been spooked or chased and had leapt into the boat by accident, trying to escape. Despite the mess I was pleased it had been returned alive – I couldn't have eaten one and it would have been a tragedy to kill such a fish or watch it die helplessly. Dorados had become part of my life now.

As sunrise flamed the eastern horizon, I was already pulling on the oars, over a dozen dorados still cruising around the boat. If it hadn't been for that slight fishy smell I could easily have thought the night's happening was all in my imagination.

With the sun revealing its full morning glory, I stopped to take a quick fix on my position. I was just short of the week's target, but there were several hours until the noon fix. Pointlessly I'd become slightly obsessed by the need to achieve or even improve the target, so I continued to row hard until midday, pulling with all my strength, sweat beading on my forehead and rolling into my eyes, hands hot and sweaty baking in their leather gloves. The sun was sucking the moisture right out of me, and with little wind conditions were sticky. I promised myself that if I'd beaten the target then I'd celebrate by jumping over the side and cleaning the hull. If only I'd brought champagne.

I clock-watched right up to twelve o'clock, the competitive streak in me overriding the enjoyment of the row itself. I was pretty sure that the last few hours' effort would have taken me further than the target, but the proof would be in the final cross drawn on the chart, marking the end of the eighth week. Just before the hour I hurriedly stowed the oars and slid into the cabin to switch the GPS on and grab the fix. I jotted down the positions from the GPS and let out a great scream and whoop of release. I'd beaten the target by seven miles, and it had been tough going. In reality, probably no tougher than any previous week, and doubtless no tougher than the coming weeks, but the target had driven me to an aching body, tendons taut and throbbing – I'd even given myself a new blister on hands with skin seemingly too hard and gnarled. Pleasure and pain in equal measure.

I sharpened my pencil and marked the chart with the position for the end of the week. I was now in the middle of the Atlantic. *Solo*, a thousand miles from anywhere. I could open the dividers to measure 1,000 nautical miles, place one point on the cross, then draw a full circle without touching any land. Wow, that was a great feeling! Could I really be a thousand miles from anywhere? In any direction? I double-checked it with a huge self-satisfied smirk on my face. This was the purest of reasons for crossing an ocean. An absolutely gob-smacking sense of being free. Just me, a tiny speck of humanity and insignificant in the universe – but I had my freedom, my fleeting moment that I couldn't capture but would remember forever. And deep in my soul a thought nudged my consciousness. Once tasted, I'd want this feeling again. This moment of freedom was not a lone pinnacle. It was but one pinnacle in a whole mountain range of them. I knew I'd need to find it again in a different place. I went back out on deck and looked around me. Most of us are shackled from an early age in a society or culture that shapes and forms us to cage our sense of wanderlust. First it's our parents and grandparents, then the turn of teachers and academics. After that it's usually a job, a boss, perhaps a mortgage, maybe other personal circumstances, but they're all there to suppress our true desires, moulding us to a system and an accepted position within the hierarchy of our species. I'm not sure if this is good or not but I know that from childhood there is an obligation to conform. How lucky I felt to step over that line and taste from this dish of freedom. I wondered just how alone I was. How many ships and boats would be within my area of visible horizon? Hopefully at least three other rowing boats. And how big was that area? My little grey cells did some quick multiplication. Recalling pi's formula I calculated it as 3,140,000 square nautical miles of open ocean: a circular area into which the United Kingdom would fit thirty-three times!

Selfishly I wanted it all to myself. Three million-plus square miles! A smile ripped across my face as I experienced a strange sense of satisfaction and contentment, pleased that I could enjoy this moment of my life. I didn't want to reach the age where life stopped giving me things and started to take them away. I could have hung in that moment forever.

CHAPTER EIGHTEEN

Destination Barbados

Just a thousand miles to go

THE HEAT SOON DREW me out of the cabin and, keeping the promise I made to myself, I grabbed the scraper and jumped over the side. The instant cooling effect of the water was heavenly as I revelled in the delight of weightlessness, my body soaking in the healing qualities of the briny ocean. Confidence restored, I dived under the boat and swam down for as long as my breath allowed then looked up at *Solo*, my pleasure tinged with an acute awareness of possible danger posed by hungry sharks. After five minutes' relaxation I started the job of scraping the hull.

The dorados were getting used to me now, and while in the water some of the bigger ones had been approaching to within a couple of metres. I held a serious amount of eye contact from one, seemingly more curious than the others, and wondered if it would be possible to get close enough to touch it. I swam away from the boat and stretched out towards the fish but it backed off just enough to keep a safe distance, then let out a jet of green fluid full of bits that clouded the water. Another first for me, being shat on by a dorado. Ah well, so much for cross-species communication, so on with the scraping.

Within the hour I was back on deck, refreshed with a cup of tea and a well-deserved slab of chocolate flapjack.

I was still on a high from beating the target I'd set for the week. I thought it well deserved so congratulated myself out loud. I was actually glad to be starting another week, my ninth, which would see me well past the halfway mark I'd crossed a couple of days ago. Now with a lighter boat and favourable winds, progress ought to be much improved, and I was looking forward to marking further positions on the left side of the chart and seeing the western side of the north Atlantic, identifying possible destinations and beginning to count down the days to the end. Briefly I indulged in anticipated success before bringing my emotions back under control. As the previous night had shown, anything can and does happen at sea!

The afternoon was tiring, windless with relentless ninety-degree heat and treacle seas that glued any forward motion. Even after my refreshing dip in the sea I felt drained, and the rowing session was merciless, the sun reflecting off the calm surface adding to the uncomfortable conditions. The priority was to make more freshwater as I was nearly out. I'd been drinking a lot, litre after litre, my body draining sweat like a colander. The heat and constant exertion fatigued me, leaving me drawn and breathless, so I escaped to the sanctuary of the cabin. Just to avoid the direct sun for a few minutes offered some relief, even though the cabin was unbearably hot.

As I lay exhausted I noticed some oil-like substance in the cabin and discovered that fluid was leaking out of the main compass. I wondered whether it was actually being boiled by the intense heat. I mopped it up hoping there'd be no more loss. The compass was essential for keeping a steady course, and although I'd a spare handheld unit it wasn't ideal, being just for emergencies. The main compass had lost about a third of its fluid but appeared to be working fine. I checked it against the handheld just to make sure. I would soon be disoriented without the boat compass, relying on it as constant confirmation that I was heading where I needed to be going. True, I had the GPS unit, but the compass was like a trusted old friend, always within vision and not requiring batteries. Deep ocean has no signs, predetermined points or anything to fix your gaze on, even stars at night would give only an approximate direction. I stayed in the cabin for an extended break, suspecting I'd got a touch of sunstroke, just using the hour to re-hydrate myself with cool, freshly desalinated water. I couldn't remember the last time I'd taken an hour off from daylight rowing: then again it had never been that hot before. Assuaging my guilt, I promised to do a night row to make up for it. I dozed off for a few minutes aware that a thumping headache was on the way. I continued drinking water and resting until darkness approached, then feeling much better decided to make the most of the downtime by doing some self-maintenance.

Out came the clippers and scissors for a long-overdue haircut. It was a welcome relief as the evening drew in the cooler air, made better by firing up the jet boil to avail myself of a luxurious hot-water shave. This was followed by a bowl of fresh warm water, lathering myself all over, then rinsing off with half a gallon of precious fresh water: the amazing recuperative powers of simple hot water. This was just what the doctor ordered and I felt back to my own self again. I prepared my evening meal of pasta on another calm night, feeling refreshed and tucking into a hearty meal.

The plan was to wait for my dinner to digest, then make up for the few hours off with a night row session, but latent exhaustion kicked in and it wasn't until midnight that I got on the oars. It was a glorious night, and, once my eyes fully adjusted, a warming blanket of stars rewarded them. I gazed up, scanning the ones that seemed to flicker slightly more than the others. My late mum always said she would be watching over me as a twinkling star, a typical mother comforting to the very end. Although she'd died many years before, those words returned and momentarily overcame me, as deep down I was still sorrowed by her death. I wasn't particularly morbid, just aware that Mum would know from my love of the outdoors that I'd sit under these stars one night and marvel, believing that they would always be there bidding me safely on my way. I saw two dancing and shimmering together, viewing them as my mum and dad looking down on me. I took comfort from that thought.

The rowing was fantastic. Although I'd done some night rowing before, tonight was special. The new moon appeared showing her narrow waxing crescent, the Sultan's moon, my dad would always say. I rowed with renewed vigour, everything different yet everything still the same. The dorados were in a squadron-like formation, appearing ghostly and pale, but clearly visible and keeping immaculate pace with the rowing. The sea so flat I could have rowed with my eyes closed. The speed was good as was the cooling night air, just perfect, and a welcome change from the heat of the day. I didn't want to stop, knowing that nights like these were rare. Individual and memorable: a solo adventurer alone as could be, owning the ocean, at one with the universe, knowing that this was yet another unique moment that would be remembered long after the journey was over. After four and a half hours I slackened the pace, energy depleted. I stowed my oars, said goodnight to my stars and retired to the cabin, barely removing my gloves before collapsing into a deep, contented sleep.

Midweek the wind picked up, nature's own air conditioning taking some of the heat out of the sun with its freshness. Progress had been good, averaging over forty nautical miles west each day. Today's noon fix put me a further forty-four miles closer to my destination, and after several hours studying the pilot books and charts I decided to make for Barbados, realising that this had probably always been my intention. I'd been to the island several times by boat and knew it well, confident that I could navigate, even in the dark if necessary, into Carlisle Bay on the southwest of the island, or Port St Charles on the northwest. The currents flow fast around Barbados, as a huge body of Atlantic water squeezes around it. The east coast is rocky and dangerous, the trade winds blowing directly onto it, so careful navigation would be required. If I came too close too soon *Solo* would be smashed up on the rocks; not close enough and I'd miss the island altogether and have to make for the Grenadines or St Lucia, a further 100 miles to the west. It was still too early to be getting hung up on landfall but today was Elaine's birthday and I wanted to give her my destination when I called later to give her my love and best wishes.

I was holding a steady course of 285 degrees compass throughout the afternoon and still pleased with progress. By the end of the week I'd be less than a thousand miles from Barbados. That may not sound like much but after battling 2,000-plus miles already I felt I was entering the final leg of my journey. I could start to countdown, even be bold enough to work out a possible estimated time of arrival, or would that be too presumptuous? No. I needed and deserved to have an end goal. At the end of this week I'd work out when I'd be back on dry land.

Just as I was thinking about all this, a huge splash at the front of the boat spun my head, flashing thoughts of a shark attack springing me into action as I stood up and quickly stowed the oars. Now blasé, I needn't have concerned myself, it was just a blue marlin. 'Ha, just a blue marlin,' I said out loud. It was enthralling to glimpse this master of the oceans, again awed as this wild predator unleashed its hunting power, a solid mass of killer muscle. I watched as it agitated around the boat, then I spotted a dorado at the stern near the rudder. It was clearly injured but the marlin was too wary of the boat to come and finish it off. I reached for the video camera, just pointing it in the general direction of the dorado, as I wanted to catch this moment with my eyes not through the viewfinder. The marlin edged ever closer, coming in for the kill, and I could sense each impatient turn and circling of the boat that bought it ever near. The dorado clung on to the final seconds of life, *Solo* offering a last tiny delay to the inevitable. I leaned over the back of the boat just a few metres from the dying fish, camera trained, but not caring if I captured the moment or not. This was nature in the raw and I wanted to experience it firsthand. The marlin overcame its wariness, took a huge turn in the water, grabbed the slowing fish, shook it in the air and swallowed it headfirst. A few more brisk and angry-looking movements and it disappeared into the deep. I remained dumbstruck at what had been played out before me. An amazing spectacle. I bowed my head slightly, not just in awe of the event but in recognition that my dorado shoal had been so viciously reduced. I played back the camera and was pleased that I had some pretty good footage, though nothing like the real-life event I'd been lucky to witness.

Still re-living the attack, I fired up the jet boil and made a brew, flicking on the desalinator to make more fresh water. I wanted to keep my three one-gallon containers full, as I was going to change the filters before the final row session of the day. I'd been putting this off, as the last couple of filter changes had caused the leak on the main filter to get worse. I had few spares and needed to be careful to avoid over-tightening the plastic filter housing. It wouldn't take much to split it, thus rendering the water maker useless. Fortunately the leak was on the low-pressure side of the system, so I hoped it would be manageable for the rest of the journey, even if it did become worse. In a damaged state it would still be better than spending an hour a day hand pumping! The filter was stained with a build-up of bacteria, which I felt explained the slight soapy taste to recent litres of water I'd been drinking.

I managed the filter change but not without apprehension. Undoing the housing was nerve-racking as it seemed excessively tight and was a battle even to get off. Eventually it succumbed and with a new filter inserted I replaced it and tightened it up all I dared. As suspected, it leaked more than ever but was manageable, though mopping up the spillage was a bit of a pain. Still, the fresh water tasted good.

With the job done I was soon back on the oars for the final evening row. I chose an album for the iPod, then eased into the now familiar rhythm of rowing. Mood played a huge part in music selection, as did tempo. Each morning on wakening up, then having breakfast, I always selected a podcast from the hundreds I'd downloaded before leaving home. It was good to hear a human voice – so many of the downloads involved lively debates or programmes that demanded concentration, taking my mind off the inevitable pain to come. The first row would be accompanied by upbeat music and always included a few favourites such as the Beatles or the Stones – they just seemed to be able to get me into the swing of it more. Strange because I'd never been a massive fan of either group, but out here they were most welcome. Afternoon sessions would find me with an eclectic range, anything and everything, just random artists or groups that I fancied after one of their songs grabbed my attention. The evening row was different again and I would always listen to Andrea Bocelli's *Vivere* album, an all-time favourite and a treat I never seemed to tire of. He would be followed with something more akin to pop to liven me up for that last push at the oars, with Avril Lavigne becoming another firm favourite despite the teenage lyrics. Not quite the sea shanties of yesteryear but a necessary routine all the same, matching my mood and the rhythm of my environment. I usually made the evening meal in the company of Michael Bublé or some other easy style as I began my day's wind-down. With over 10,000 tracks to choose from, and listening to the iPod for about twenty hours a day, it was a vital piece of equipment I would sorely have missed. Having an iPod amplifier and fixed waterproof external speakers was an excellent decision when constructing *Solo*. It was quite amusing to reflect that even with my desire for freedom from social controls I couldn't escape the routines and patterns that came from the music.

I set up the satellite phone, called Elaine and wished her a happy birthday. I'd previously arranged for flowers to be delivered, which seemed the least I could do. It was a long call and we chatted about what had been happening in general and what the boys had been up to, though I couldn't escape the feeling that I was just down the road and would be back in an hour or so. In truth I'd now been at sea for sixty-one days, ten weeks since I'd left home. I told her that I was making for Barbados as a destination and would call Bradley, our elder son, on Friday to give him an ETA. Friday was Bradley's birthday and I'd promised him I'd call him before he went to school. I think this was the first time I'd ever been away for a family birthday and it felt distinctly odd. Our chatter eventually tailed off and we said our goodbyes, my cabin reverting to its usual quietness together with that strange sense of loneliness that is so often the result of a long phone call. I'd enjoyed a good chat and realised how much I was missing a decent conversation.

I took a fix and wrote up my log:

Time, 2245. Wind, E2. Heading, 290 degrees compass. Comment, everything is nothing if you have no one to share it with.

Chapter Nineteen

Milestones and turning points

Every day closer would mean one day less

I'D BEEN UP FOR several hours already. The sun was still below the horizon but the stars were fading and dawn would creep through before too long. I went outside to set up the aerial for the satellite phone. I was still working to Greenwich Mean Time (now called Universal Time), which meant sunrise would be about 0915 hours. I'd promised to call Bradley with an ETA so my early start was to ensure that everything was ready to make the call just after 0800.

I'd passed the 1,000-miles-to-go target two days earlier and knew that by the noon fix today I'd have just over 900 nautical miles west left to Barbados. Today was Friday and the end of week nine. Nine whole weeks at sea. Another small chunk completed and I was already anticipating the noon fix to add another cross on the chart, edging ever closer to landfall. I'd done some rough calculations for Bradley and reckoned on another twenty-three more days, giving me an ETA in Barbados of 7th April. That would require an average daily mileage of forty miles, but I sensed I'd find another gear and step up the pace for a sprint finish, assuming of course the weather stayed settled. The para anchor had been stowed for a few weeks now and I reckoned I wouldn't need it again now I was firmly in the trade winds. I rather hoped I'd be able to shave a few days of the ETA and get there in under three weeks, but I'd tell Bradley the 7th and hope for the best.

I made the call and explained to my excited son that I'd be in Barbados on 7th April, just over three weeks away. It seemed such a short while to me but for a nine-year-old probably an age. I reassured him that I was trying my best and would call him and Joel again the following week. Elaine then updated me on the other three rowing boat positions.

Matt and Alan in the pair's boat, who had set off a few hours before me, were about 150 miles to the east of my position. We'd been in similar weather patterns and at one time were over 300 miles apart, both boats being pushed south by the strong northerlies, but now on track for landfall in Barbados. I doubted they would be able to catch me up and, appealing to my competitive edge, I didn't want them to either. Anthony and Sam in their boats were some 200-odd miles to the north of me and heading for Antigua. They'd experienced different weather conditions and expected to hit land a few days before me. We were close to each other in relative terms but still miles apart. Distances over the last few weeks had been in the thousands, but now they'd be in the hundreds.

The morning session was one long row of three hours. It was great to be on the oars watching the sun come up, and yet I started to feel that familiar tinge of sadness that comes as each adventure ends. I could now measure the time left at sea by successive sunrises, so few left. Every day closer would mean one day less, regret and relief coming together, swirling and mingling, fighting for dominance in my thoughts. I knew I'd leave a part of me out here in the ocean as I'd done on every other voyage. With the end in sight I didn't want to leave my zone, the little part of the world I'd called my own, at the same time knowing I couldn't stay, the bittersweet condition of the human soul, always moving on, always wanting to remain. I shook away the thoughts of journey's end – it would come soon enough and I'd deal with that when I had to. What wouldn't go away was the sickening reality that getting back to 'normality' was maybe going to be harder than I'd imagined.

The noon fix confirmed my estimations and at the end of week nine I was 903 miles east of Barbados. Excitement welled up in my stomach. I was on the final countdown. My watch read a quarter past twelve. Time to get back on the oars. Sunset would be about 2115 and that meant another nine hours' rowing.

The weekend went well, each day knocking off over forty miles. By Monday's noon fix I'd have between 750 and 800 miles left. The weather remained settled, though the wind alternated between nothing and slight breezes. I didn't mind. I drank plenty of water, kept my hat on and focused on the rowing. Once I'd got the rhythm of each session, the hours leaked into days and every one brought that ETA closer.

I had also been giving myself the odd treat of cooling breaks in the water. I usually jumped in about the hottest part of the day for a relaxing ten minutes swimming, a pleasant change to stretch out in thousands of square miles of ocean instead of a cramped boat. The hull no longer needed scraping, though I wiped it down every couple of days to remove the build-up of green slime, a useful excuse for staying in the water for a few extra minutes.

I'd got to thinking that if sharks were to appear while I was in the water they'd ignore me in favour of tasty dorados, but recalling how fast these predators were I also pondered whether they'd take the easy option and go for the slowest chunk of meat around. That meant me. From then on I still enjoyed my cooling dips but returned to keeping a watchful eye out – it would have been a total waste of energy to have rowed over 2,000 miles only to finish up as fish meal! All the stripy fish had now disappeared except, unaccountably, for one. I named him Sergeant Stripy and would feed him biscuit crumbs or the odd tiny goose barnacle from the back of the boat, when I was in the water. He was a friendly little chap and would eagerly take the food from my fingers. His snacks might not last much longer though as the biscuits were becoming scarce – in fact food was actually becoming a bit of an issue. That day I'd eaten the last dehydrated breakfast meal and knew by the end of the week most of the nice things would have gone. I still had several kilos of dried pasta and noodles so wouldn't starve, but future meals would be pretty uninteresting without anything to add to them. I decided to do a full stock-take at the end of the week to see exactly what was left. With a pretty accurate ETA calculated, I could work out if I needed to start to ration myself.

On Tuesday morning, making my morning cuppa in the milky light of dawn, I noticed there were no dorados around the boat and wondered if something had spooked them. There were no flying fish, either in the water or stunned onboard, which also seemed a bit unusual. And nothing appeared all day, though I constantly scanned the horizon hoping to see them as I rowed. They were only fish but had been faithful companions for so long that I felt a kind of loneliness, still hoping they'd return. I remained fish-less all the next day as well and concluded they'd headed off for the relative safety of the empty ocean. Being only 700 miles or so from Barbados I'd soon be in fishing territory in and around the islands, with many Barbadians keen to bag a tasty dorado.

The sea seemed to have taken on a slightly different colour, slightly darker and not as clear as it had been. I wondered if that was the reason for the dorados moving on, still missing them milling around the boat – but they'd gone and that was that.

I had a visitor on Wednesday night, a pigeon-sized bird with webbed feet that took some shelter on *Solo*. The rain had been lashing down and the boat was constantly slammed by a northerly swell. The bird managed to find a quiet corner in the foot well, looking pretty wet and exhausted. It took no notice of me, tucked its head under a wing and went to sleep. It flew off in the morning once the rain had eased off. Although I never saw it again, there was evidence of return visits for a few nights as a feather or two and droppings appeared in the foot well each morning. It was nice to have a visitor, the wildlife had been pretty quiet since the dorados had moved on.

On Friday morning I awoke early again – for some reason I hadn't been sleeping well lately. It was 3.30 a.m., sunrise another six hours away. I went outside, made a brew and just sat there under a bright moon. The wind was light and although the sea was calm there was a huge northerly swell that gave the boat a lovely up-and-down motion, like being in a slow lift. I sipped the hot sweet tea, thankful that I still had a good supply of teabags, sugar and powdered milk. I couldn't help but feel that this recent restlessness and lack of sleep was due to the thought of journey's end. Noon today would mark the tenth week at sea and, much as I was looking forward to getting back with family and friends, I couldn't shake off a maudlin sentimentality. I knew I was going to miss the tranquillity, my own expanse of ocean and sipping tea.

After an hour I returned to the cabin to try and sleep again, but to no avail. A food stock-check was required so I went through all the lockers looking for everything edible. I found a handful of chocolate bars, twenty raisin flapjacks and eight main meals, a further five packets of biscuits, two large bars of chocolate, a bundle of twelve Peperami sticks and, to my great surprise, a Jamaican ginger cake — a huge saliva-inducing bonus. I carefully piled up my newfound goodies in the cabin and, together with two kilos of pasta and a large packet of noodles, that was the lot. The key decision now was how best to ration the stores or indeed whether to ration at all. Burning huge amounts of energy each day with rationed stocks would test my self-discipline to the limit, and I just knew I'd break into extra stores if hungry, so better to eat what I wanted within reason and trust to my timetable in reaching Barbados. In the end I compromised. I now had about 600 miles left. Something for breakfast was a must, so I put fifteen raisin flapjacks in the small locker, using one a day for breakfast and hopefully a few spares — that was the only rationing I'd do. Evening meals would be the important substantial meal so the pasta would accompany the dehydrated meals to bulk them up, giving me eight days of interesting meals: after that I'd be left with plain pasta and noodles.

There was no way I was going to resist the Jamaican ginger cake, so I made a coffee and duly polished it off, savouring every delicious crumb. Dawn was now less than an hour away and I was keen to get rowing, looking forward to the noon fix and the end of week ten. Placing the weekly cross on the chart was an enjoyable task, seeming to confirm that all the exertion had been worthwhile, that symbolic mark tangible evidence of real progress. Noon soon arrived and the cross was duly marked. I'd rowed 282 miles further west, leaving me about 580 miles or so to go. I could almost taste the cool beer that was awaiting me. I reworked my ETA and calculated that 5th April would do it, two days better than the previous estimate. Another two weeks if I really push myself, I reckoned. Mentally I felt strong and I just hoped the body would be as willing.

Friday afternoons were always a bit of an anticlimax. Once the noon fix had been taken it was like starting the working week all over again – a lifetime of social conditioning to live within a cycle of seven days was still very difficult to lose. Still, my target was drawing nearer with every pull so I returned to the task, iPod on, mind switched off and back in the routine. The afternoon flew past – only another six days to the end of the next week.

I devoured the evening meal of shepherd's pie mixed in with a big bowl of pasta, a strange sort of concoction, but it certainly did the trick. The pasta remnants would serve as the next day's snack and would help conserve the rapidly dwindling supply of chocolate bars. After the meal I made my usual coffee and sat in the cabin listening to music. It had been another hard day and the restless sleep patterns of the last few nights were starting to take effect. I hoped tonight I would get a sound five to six hours, so needed this preparatory relaxation. Soon enough I was fighting to stay awake. My watch said 12.30 so I flicked off the light and lay down in a pleasantly exhausted state. Finally I slept well and although waking up several times I was quickly returned to a deep sleep.

Eight o'clock came soon enough and I knew I had a good hour before it would be light enough to row. For some time now getting up in the morning was a ritual I would have preferred to ignore. Each day my hands would be curled up claw-like and I'd have to work out the stiffness in order to get up and start the morning's routine. After weeks of physical exertion, legs, arms, joints and tendons were taut to snapping point and the constant shifts of movement and non-movement created intense pain that required much mental effort to overcome. The temptation just to wake and remain motionless, knowing that just getting up would incur waves of agony, was, at times, so overwhelming that it took several minutes to convince myself that there really was no other option. My supply of anti-inflammatory tablets was steadily reducing, I'd little idea whether they were doing any good but the alternative, not taking them, was too big a risk for me. With a grunt and a grimace, I'd force myself out of the bunk, reach for the tablets then crawl in search of the jet boil and a brew of tea – my great lifesaver. Once downed with one of the precious raisin flapjacks, I would be ready to start the day. Twenty minutes on the oars, the pain would ease and like a well-oiled if somewhat knackered steam engine I would methodically pull away, stroke after stroke, hour after hour, westward bound towards the setting sun.

I was rowing well and conditions were perfect, the wind a good force-four northeasterly, with sunshine. In a light mood of contentment the days leaked into each other with some good mileage gained. Over the weekend I totalled 93 miles, with Monday and Tuesday adding 102 miles west, averaging well over the 40-mile-a-day target I'd set myself. I knew that by Wednesday I'd break into the 400 miles remaining, and that would mean possibly just nine days to go. Mentally I knew I could do it, and what my brain ordered I knew my body could deliver. I would have plenty of time to recover once I had the crossing in the bag, so I allowed myself to welcome the anticipation and excitement: a dream was coming to fruition, a project nearing its completion. I was excited, it felt good. In some ways the next day would be just like every other, but it would also be another milestone, a turning point. Single-figure days left to go and a growing taste of success. I wanted to achieve this adventure now more than ever, especially after all the physical and mental effort and the strain it had placed on my family. Although this project was coming to, hopefully, a successful conclusion, there would be another one. I knew it. I didn't want to wake up one morning wondering what had happened to my life: I wanted to keep waking up and wonder what else I could do.

Chapter Twenty

Mixed emotions

I pulled as hard as I could into the darkening sky

WEDNESDAY'S NOON FIX CONFIRMED I'd rowed a further 41 miles west, leaving me a distance left to run of 385. If conditions stayed fair and in my favour, then that meant some time within seven to nine days I'd be sitting in a quiet bar with a cool bottle of beer, with as much fresh food as I could eat, listening to the chatter in Caribbean patois. Those thoughts drove me back to the oars and gave me further reason to strive on, the relentless push for Barbados and the safety of the harbour. My twisted and mauled body could then rest and recover, but not yet. There were still plenty of sea miles left and I really needed to focus, digging deep with every stroke. Achieving over fifty miles west each day was akin to back-to-back marathons, and I found myself rowing as hard as possible.

That afternoon I spotted a sailing yacht on the horizon. I couldn't remember the last time I'd seen a vessel of any sort, certainly weeks and weeks ago. The boat was a good sign that I was getting closer to land. It remained in my sight for a good part of the day but eventually grew smaller and disappeared, the small white dot vanishing as though it had never been there. I suddenly felt incredibly lonely, ridiculous really since the yacht I'd seen had been miles away, but a sadness descended, leaving me and *Solo* alone again. It made me realise just how much I was missing human companionship, and a part of me wanted the boat to have been nearer, close enough for a conversation. I'd started this journey because I wanted my version of freedom, which included time alone, but we humans are gregarious by instinct. Very few people truly are islands.

The weather had turned a bit squally by Wednesday night and the unsettled conditions continued throughout Thursday. The squalls were violent, I would see them building on the horizon for ages, then all of a sudden the wind would gust and moments later I'd be engulfed in a torrent of ferocious, heavy, biting rain. They were short-lived but enormously intense, one shredding my flag, blowing bits of red ensign cotton everywhere. The Atlantic takes on a different mood in those conditions: the sea changes to black and the air turns cool and heavy as powerful winds rip spray into the air from breaking crests. Swathes of rain sweep in and everything disappears from view as the whole atmosphere becomes cloaked in satanic turmoil. Fortunately squalls don't last long and are usually over as quickly as they come. Then the next one begins to build in the distance and the cycle is repeated. In some ways I quite like them, though they disrupt the rowing momentum. There's something quite primeval about huddling in a cabin at the mercy of the elements, a little frisson of fear, but knowing it will soon be over and almost looking forward to the next one – a bit like a short-lived roller coaster. They're also a good excuse for a ten-minute break to seek shelter and make a brew. Conditions remained similar throughout the night but I slept through the worst and by morning the sky was clear once again, the bad weather having blown through. Quite a confused sea had been left behind, but flattening out as the morning progressed. Nothing could dampen my spirits this morning, as it was Friday once more. I was keen to get the noon fix, a big occasion most days, but Friday was the day to mark the full week's progress. This Friday was special and celebratory – it might just be the last one!

Noon was slow to come as I clock-watched all morning, and it took an enormous amount of willpower to keep going right up to midday. A watched clock never speeds, to mix a metaphor. Bang on noon I stowed the oars and got the fix from the GPS. What a relief! It had been a great week's rowing, totalling 331 miles further west, with daily runs of 42, 51, 50, 52, 41, 50, and today's 45. I did the calculations. I was now 290 miles east of Barbados. If I pushed hard I could be there for next Thursday, just six days left. I wrote up the log and then went back out to the oars, the usual Friday afternoon anticlimax pushed away by a renewed vigour and energy. I took up the initial strain, then slowly built up speed until I'd reached my normal rhythm. Firmly back in gear, I leant back into the pull then heard an almighty crack. The seat stopped dead as I carried on and fell off, arms and legs flailing like a madman as I sought to prevent damage to myself and the oars. One of the axles for the seat wheels had snapped, the first one to go since leaving La Gomera eleven weeks earlier. The initial dismay was soon tempered as I rummaged around the spares locker and eventually pulled out a new one. There was no other equipment damage so within a few minutes I was back hard at it, with just a slight bruise for my troubles. I don't need gear failure now, I thought, not when I'm so close.

The afternoon sped past and by sunset I was pleased with the day's effort and celebrated with a chomp on some Peperami sticks while I boiled some pasta. The desire to conserve my limited rations got no further than my brain. At the end of each day I was simply ravenous and reckoned with only a handful of days left I'd be okay.

After the meal I sat on deck sipping coffee, enjoying the reflective moment and feeling quite pleased with myself. I'd survived eleven whole weeks at sea, punishing my body and mind daily. I'd expected the journey to be tough, but the perception of toughness before any event is never the same as the reality. I'd expected pain and dark days – I'd been there and done it on my previous Atlantic solo sail, but rowing was a new challenge and I'd had no prior experience to learn from, so yes, it had been tough, though I was exceptionally pleased with the way I'd handled the mental side of things. Eleven weeks had been a long time with no human contact, other than an occasional sat-phone call. Feeling low and striking up one-way conversations with fish and birds was inevitable but acceptable. I couldn't get *eleven weeks* out of my head. *Eleven whole sodding weeks*: a year in the planning, eleven weeks in the execution. I thought back to childhood and the six-week summer break from school: how long that had seemed at the time, with the countless things that I'd managed to cram in. Here I was doing the equivalent of two summer holidays, which would make future fortnight family holidays seem short. I finished the rest of my coffee and turned in for the night. A new tomorrow beckoned, a final countdown that would bring me ever closer to the end.

Friday's run of 47 miles put me 243 miles east of Barbados, when I took Saturday's noon fix. I set a mini-target for the afternoon to push myself harder, and when I reached it I challenged myself to do an extra three miles before I could stop for dinner. With the sun just dropping behind the horizon I pulled as hard as I could into the darkening sky and was exhausted when I finally ended the day. I felt weak with hunger and it didn't take long for the rest of the Peperami sticks to fall victim to my rumbling stomach, as I sat with the jet boil between my legs, cooking pasta. Out of the blue a garfish suddenly jumped out of the sea and into the boat. Still gripping onto the stove, I managed to get the fish back into the water – at about a foot long it would have made a tasty meal, but I was happy to release it. I had sufficient basic food for my needs and it would have been callous merely to eat it because I could. Live and let live, eh? I used to catch garfish by the score when I lived in Saudi Arabia as a boy. They were a favourite delicacy of the local Lebanese shopkeeper, and half a dozen good-sized specimens would guarantee me a few packets of sweets for my efforts.

Again I slept well on a full stomach, hardly waking at all during the night, and when I did it was straight back to sleep. The next morning seemed harder than usual – clearly the extra exertion had punished my body, which was also particularly stiff through lack of movement while I slept. Noon fixes were now daily fixations and my mornings were consumed with clock-watching. Another 49 miles done, only 194 to go. Keep rowing, Dave, keep rowing. I wrote in my log that I needed to focus and dig deeper, as if writing it down would help me find that extra bit of push. I looked down at my body, long stripped of any excess fat, and realised my energy consumption was eating into my muscles, wasting me slowly away bit by bit. Somewhere in the back of my mind a small, still voice tried unsuccessfully to remind me that I was here to find freedom from timescales and targets and objectives. I was here to marvel, to wonder, to experience an environment I'd yearned for so long to be a part of. Surely, it kept trying to say, that mindset should last the distance. Enjoy it, Dave, let it last, savour every precious moment. But that voice was drowned out in the clamour to finish, to meet my self-appointed deadline. My sights were set on the Barbadian finishing line and I wanted an end to it. As the whole project had consumed me in the early days of boat design and funding, so the endgame had begun to tear large chunks from my passion just 'to be'. My competitive edge was crowding out my higher esoteric intentions. Without fully realising it, I was racing desperately to get back to the human race. I looked round *Solo* and felt proud that she had got me this far. She still looked good and seemed to be saying, 'I'm holding up better than you.' Jamie had certainly done a good job, and the bond I felt with the boat in the workshop was now fully rounded. No longer was *I* crossing the ocean, *we* were a team working together. I patted the top of the locker that I used as the chart table in grateful acknowledgment, a sort of thanks to my boat and all who'd been involved with her.

I'd been daydreaming. Time was slipping by, yet I already felt exhausted. Another nine hours to row, I mumbled to myself as I clambered out of the hatch. The sun was hot and I found myself wishing for squalls to get some respite from the relentless heat. I declared that the next break, in about two and a half hours, would be a swim break. It usually became unbearably hot in the middle part of the day before the trade winds pick up in the afternoon with their cooling breezes.

The row session went well and with *Solo* light and riding high we made good progress, even though the sea was fairly choppy. It was a little too rough for a swim really, but the thought of that cool water and a good body stretch was irresistible. I tied on my safety rope and dived in. *Solo* was bucking about in the swell so I swam a few metres away to avoid being knocked out by my own boat – very unprofessional! It felt weird to look at *Solo* being thrown around, and suddenly I was very aware of being alone treading water in the depths of a huge ocean. Some sort of sixth sense mixed in with *déjà vu* told me this was unsafe. It was probably nothing but tiredness and the roughness of the sea but, trusting my instincts, I didn't stay in the water too long and was back on deck. As I looked up, I was amazed to see a huge cargo ship heading straight for me, barely a couple of miles away. I grabbed the handheld VHF radio and quickly flicked it to Channel 16, the international marine channel for emergencies.

'Green cargo ship, green cargo ship,' I said, trying to appear calm. 'This is boat *Positive Outcomes*, boat *Positive Outcomes*. Off your starboard bow, do you read me? Over.'

The captain came on and said that yes, he'd spotted me, and where was I bound? I replied that I was heading for Barbados and that it was good to know I was visible from the ship's bridge, especially as his decks were stacked with containers. He wished me safe passage and ended the transmission. The radio fell silent and I watched, as his boat steamed ever closer, to within a quarter of a mile, then past and into the distance. I made a brew as I watched her grow smaller, admitting after the event that it had been a little light entertainment while it lasted. I rummaged in the locker for some biscuits. Food stocks were now almost gone and today would see the last of snacks and anything nice. Tomorrow would be pasta with dried milk and sugar. I could hardly wait!

Monday's noon fix put me 149 miles east of Barbados. I wrote in large capitals in my log, STAY FOCUSED!!! My body was struggling with the pace and with the lack of high-calorie snacks – my energy levels felt depleted. I still had a full bag of sugar left and was adding several scoops to my drinks, which seemed to help as a pick-me-up during the day. The thought of being so close to the island kept me going and I was relying on Tuesday's noon fix to calculate the time I'd be arriving. The timing was important as I wanted to get to harbour in daylight if possible, being a lot safer than in the depths of night. The wind was beginning to strengthen from the north, pushing me south, and movement in this direction would increase, especially at night when I would not be rowing, so I'd have to make the decision on Tuesday whether to continue my course for the northern end of the island or run south. Tomorrow was therefore a key decision point, not critical but important. What I did was down to distance, weather and how I felt about my physical capabilities and state of mind.

I'd seen a few ships on the horizon throughout the day and a few telltale lights the previous night. My ownership of the ocean was shrinking as the outside world crowded in. There now seemed to be ships everywhere, which initially seemed rather strange, as I hadn't seen any for most of my crossing. I wasn't unduly concerned about them, the chances of being run down were minimal, but I'd have been pretty annoyed if such an event had occurred so close to finishing. Then again, being hit full on by a ship doing twenty-plus knots per hour would not have left me with much time to express regret or disappointment.

I rowed hard all day, fighting the wind and trying not to lose too much ground to the south. There wasn't much I could do about slippage during the night, but it was frustrating as I monitored progress on the GPS, sipping hot sweet tea and waiting for daylight, willing the wind to ease. Despite exhaustion, I didn't feel like sleeping. Thoughts of finishing, of being swept too far south, of being driven onto the dangerous eastern rocky shore of Barbados, all conspired to keep my mind more or less alert. I dozed rather than slumbered. I was in the endgame, apprehension and excitement competing for my attention.

The day's run at Tuesday's noon fix put me fifty-four miles closer to Barbados. It was now 1st April and I'd broken into a new month. I harked back to Friday 11th January in La Gomera, such a long time ago when I'd loosed the lines and slipped away. A large chunk of my life crammed into eighty days – had I really been at sea for that long? The noon fix taken, I was back on the oars barely ten minutes after plotting my position. I slurped a quick snatch of tea, then returned to the seat, straining to combat a stiff wind on my port stern, rowing hard. I took a few more short breaks throughout the day, but obsessed with losing ground I found they were short indeed. The weather continued to run me south so I took the decision. The way the currents and wind were colluding I knew I needed to hit the south side of the island, though even that was going to be at the expense of much exhaustion. I took regular GPS quick fixes throughout the afternoon, to give me an idea of how things were progressing – I'd plot them on the chart later. I was now gripped by the overwhelming desire to finish the day after next, an achievable goal but ridiculous within the context of my overall journey. I'd so longed to escape life's restrictions, yet here I was beating myself up to get back to them. But the finish line was tantalisingly close and thoughts of home, family, cool beers, a decent shower and a hot meal, overrode everything. Man is frail indeed when home comforts tread on high ideals. However, I was in the zone and needed to make mileage. The cross-swell and wind were awful companions, wilfully toying with me like a plaything, a cornered mouse to their cat. Rowing took enormous concentration, not ideal, but I was overcome with the closeness of victory. I could taste it, just a couple of days, Dave, come on! I wrote in large capitals in my log, HARD-HARD-HARD…DIG DEEP, DAVE. FOCUS!!

I rowed into the dark night in near impossible conditions, struggling for an hour or so. The wind was really up now, gusting as I took shelter in the cabin with a well-earned brew. It had picked up quickly and was now blowing a good force-six, the sea increasingly swept with treacherous-looking waves racing out of the blackness. Part of the problem was I was coming into a relative shallow, and the waves were heaping up water from the vast ocean depths, cramming huge volumes into a smaller area. *Solo* was constantly lifted and slewed around, now dangerously light for such a rough sea. My freshly made hot brew spilt everywhere as *Solo* keeled right over on a breaking wave. She hung in that moment of balance and I braced myself to be fully rolled, but she sat back down as the wave went through. I struggled outside to check everything was secure then flooded the ballast tank to give the boat a little more stability. Part of me regretted the necessity of adding weight as I watched gallons of water flood into the tank, but better a stable craft than a watery grave. Once full, I rammed the plug back in and made another quick brew – this one I managed to drink.

Conditions were dangerous for lighting the jet boil for cooking pasta, but energy was needed for the next day. My plan was to start in the dark, about six in the morning if I could, but, as ever, sea conditions would determine the day.

Two o'clock in the morning and still I hadn't slept. There was no point in getting undressed, I just lay there listening, as I had so many times, to the waves battering *Solo*, marvelling at her resilience and the skill of those who had built her. It seemed grossly unfair that the elements could conspire against me at this late stage, so close and all that, but the sea doesn't give up victory easily: maybe I'd been too presumptuous and I'd be blown further south, missing the island altogether. Too many thoughts, no solutions, powerless against nature's forces, and nothing I could do about it. Sleep still wouldn't come so out I went for another brew. If I'd had a pound for every brew I'd made on this voyage I'd be a rich man indeed, I thought. But I was rich, not financially, but infinitely richer within my soul and my experiences. Hard to feel privileged when facing an ocean's battering, but would I have missed it? I had no doubt as to the answer.

As if in affirmation that I'd given the gods the correct answer, the cloud cleared somewhat and I could make out the glow from Barbados far away on the horizon. Wow, it felt so close – roll on the morning so I could get on the oars again! I sat in the cockpit, swathed in my waterproofs, sipping hot sweet drinks and gazing at the looming light. It was mesmerising, staring at my destination while wishing away the dark. Returning to the cabin I slipped on some sleep-inducing music and eventually dropped off for an hour or so. The next time I glanced at my watch it was just after five in the morning.

Sea conditions were still the same. I decided to give it an hour or so then empty the ballast tank and have a go at rowing. In the meantime more sweet drinks would boost the energy I knew I was going to need. At seven a.m. I set up the oars, but it was hopeless. Still dark with a running sea I just couldn't find any rhythm at all. After a brief but futile struggle I admitted defeat, retired to the cabin and waited for daybreak. To have carried on would have wasted precious energy and likely have risked snapping an oar.

Sufficient light leaked through at about nine. I was already on the seat, waiting impatiently, fearing I would have to abandon a further attempt, but with some hard rowing I quickly had the pattern of the sea and rowed furiously. Checking my position in relation to Barbados, I reckoned I had somewhere around the forty-five-mile mark to reach the harbour.

After two relentless hours I took a fix and, looking west, spotted land. There was no sense of jubilation or journey's end, just focused, mechanical concern, a matter-of-fact calculation that I needed to keep on a steady course, not crab south and miss the island. The GPS was now on permanently, providing constant updates to aid navigation. I'd also been plotting the fixes on a larger-scale chart, showing Barbados a couple of inches long, rather than the tiny spec on the ocean chart I had been staring at for the last few weeks.

The wind had swung round to the east by midday and was no longer gusty. This made rowing so much easier, and when the sun came out my morale went up several notches and I began to look forward to a great afternoon. Already I could pick out buildings on the island, the cue for a wave of anxiety to dissipate. Although I consider myself a competent ocean navigator, there's nothing like tangible proof of solid land, especially the right piece of land, to aid the onset of a more relaxed state. I felt confident that I had the energy to get to Bridgetown Harbour that evening, a quick check of the GPS and, at the current pace, I reckoned I'd make harbour before 2000 hours, enough daylight to make it safe. Setting up the satellite phone, I called Thomas, my contact in Barbados. He'd previously agreed with me to put *Solo* in Port St Charles Marina, and said if I called him with an ETA for Bridgetown he would organise a tow up the west coast to the harbour moorings.

I went back on the oars and rowed as hard as my body would manage. It felt marvellous. *Solo* was as light as she'd ever been and riding high: the thought of success drove away the usual aches and pains as I fantasised about getting up tomorrow morning and not having to row. I could lie in bed all day. I could eat salad, fresh fish, meat and fruit. I could do all these secure in the knowledge that the project had been successful. These thoughts spurred and drove me relentlessly on, as I prayed energy levels would keep up with the pace.

At two o'clock, after a GPS check, I marked my position on the large-scale chart – just over fourteen miles from South Point and the southernmost tip of Barbados. The currents ran fast around the point and there were several reefs to contend with. I needed to be careful and keep a steady course. The aim was to keep a mile off shore to pass

South Point then head northwest up to Carlisle Bay, past Bridgetown Harbour and around the back where there were moorings for small boats. Here I would meet the boat that would tow me into Port St Charles. I'd been there before when I'd completed my transatlantic sail, so was confident I could navigate the latter stages by eye. Back on the oars, I confirmed I'd already rowed nearly twenty-four miles since daybreak and reckoned I'd another twenty-two to the mooring. The afternoon was becoming increasingly hotter, so this last leg was not going to be easy. I took a long swig from my water bottle, tipped the rest over my head and neck, grabbed the oars and settled into the rhythm once more.

As the miles slipped by, Barbados grew bigger and the colourful houses on the shoreline became ever more prominent. I revelled in the close detail of the buildings and landscape, avidly searching for features of which I'd been starved for so long, craning my neck for characteristics that normally wouldn't have warranted a second glance. The usual had become the unusual, my senses having been attuned to sea and sky for so long. Land was a strange environment and the thought of rediscovering it filled with me with tired exhilaration.

I rowed past within fifty yards of a fisherman as I cleared South Point, giving him a nod, which was returned with a wave of his hand. His puzzled look at my gangly and sweating body spoke volumes, but I heroically smiled as if this was something I did every day. Altering course slightly to crab further inland, I turned northwest up to Bridgetown, feeling the currents clawing, trying to push me in the opposite direction. Hard rowing got me within half a mile of the shore and the sounds of music and general noise wafted out to greet me. Now I could see people swimming and sunbathing: I could smell food and pollution and the familiar landmarks I recognised from a few years earlier. Before long I could make out the distinctive Hilton Hotel on Needham's Point at the southern edge of Carlisle Bay, knowing that, once around the corner, it would just be a case of crossing the bay and arriving in Bridgetown Harbour. I was literally shaking and fizzing with excitement and had trouble containing myself from shouting out loud with self-congratulation. At the same time my mind couldn't quite comprehend that I'd soon be finished and the oars would be stowed for the very last time. A tinge of regret and sadness sneaked in alongside my excitement. Despite my manic desperation to finish, I knew I'd left behind another chapter of my life that I would miss deeply. Snapshots of the past year crowded in and flashed through my mind – people, places, problems, heartaches, jubilation – too many emotions to control or consider. I'd done it. I'd rowed one of the world's great oceans, solo and unaided, land to land. I'd become as one with my environment again, yet for now all those crazy, jumbled feelings would have to remain unanalysed. I was here, that was sufficient.

As I rowed across the bay and around the towering concrete walls of Bridgetown Harbour, the current was strong, requiring much effort, then, rounding the back of the harbour and sheltered from the wind, I steadied my pace. A rickety old jetty hove into view and I spotted the motorboat that would give me the tow to Port St Charles. A couple of grinning guys greeted me and passed me the towing rope. 'Welcome to Barbados, man,' they laughed. 'Just da customs, eh, den all da beer you need!'

Once in tow I set up the satellite phone and made a quick call to Elaine, feeling slightly trembly and emotional as we spoke. She was clearly relieved that I was safe and the project was over. No more worrying, I told her, and said I'd call tomorrow for a longer chat when everything was sorted. The call ended, then silence, save the chugging of the towboat and the lap of waves. It seemed very odd to be moving without being in control. A wave of tiredness threatened to engulf me as my body deflated with a big sigh. No more rowing, blisters or hardship. I looked again at the GPS information where I had stopped it at the jetty. I'd rowed 45.63 miles in ten hours and fifty-nine minutes and my body knew it.

I soon entered Port St Charles, let go the towline and rowed to the jetty. A small gathering of people from the open-air restaurant came out and gave me a round of applause, to which I responded with a modest wave and a grin. I secured the ropes to *Solo* and it finally dawned on me that it was over. I'd experienced the gamut of emotions. I'd laughed and cried, been to heaven and hell, been scared and elated beyond belief. I'd seen an ocean at its most benign and at its most destructive, seen the natural world and come to know again my strengths and frailties as a unique human being. Above all I'd experienced again what freedom means to me, an elusive elixir I knew I'd have to search for again and again. My first solo, unaided ocean row had been a challenge worth doing and ultimately achieved. Would I do it again? As I stepped ashore I had different priorities, a long beer and a slow hot shower.

A question came from the small gathering of diners. 'Is this your first rowing adventure or have you rowed before?'

I replied with a weary smile. 'Never rowed before until I had this boat...never going to row again!'

Epilogue

THE END OF MY epic adventure was not, of course, the end of the story. My first few nights in an apartment in St James Parish was a strange experience. I remember the soft sheets, the hot showers, the excellent food, and the spacious luxury, but three months in a tiny rocking boat cannot be easily forgotten. It took a while to get used to land that didn't lurch or sway. Subconsciously, I listened for the waves and the slap of the sea against the hull. I didn't miss being salt-encrusted, damp or the smell of my fetid body odour. But in a way I did. I'd become accustomed to a lifestyle and an environment that had enveloped me and taken me to its heart. I missed my dorados and stripy fish. I felt happy, sad, contented, unsettled. I kept thinking back to what I'd achieved, but I couldn't find its soul anymore. I was proud of my achievement but it was over and done with and something had left me. I wanted to recapture those heart-stopping sunsets and those feelings of aloneness. I had the memories but not their essence. It was as if there had been another Dave Clarke who'd taken the experiences and just left me the husks. I felt dismissed by the sea and the sky, like a jilted lover, confused and adrift. Sometimes I'd gaze back over that vast ocean from the beach and just feel inexplicably different. Freedom does that to me. I had spent a hard year wanting to rekindle the experience so much, while knowing it was a fleeting emotion that would slip through my fingers – as it had done so many times before. That old human condition, forever wanting to hold onto what is precious, forever wanting to keep moving on.

But another part of me was relieved – I was keen to be back with my friends and family again. The rational part of me acknowledged the challenge was over, as well I knew it had to be. My 'real' world was waiting back in Britain and I had work to do in order to return. Elaine and the boys were pleased, relieved and excited over the phone. I promised I'd be back within a week with stories and presents. I just had to get *Solo* ready for shipping back home.

The week was spent relaxing, sleeping, catching up with the world and cleaning my boat out ready for her return. It was a peculiar feeling when I put *Solo* on the trailer, ready for crating, no doubt wondering what she had done to deserve another imprisonment. It was also odd to board a plane for a journey that would take hours, not months, and as we took off I looked down on that vast blue ocean, memories hastily tumbling over themselves, not quite believing it had been me down there, endlessly rowing. A weird, almost out-of-body experience.

Solo sat on my garage drive for a few weeks, but she didn't fit. She was born for the water and deserved to be returned to it, so I offered her up for sale. She was soon sold and I hope she finds deep water again some day.

And what of my fellow-rowers? Alan and Matt in the pairs boat finally made it into Barbados some four days after me, but had to be towed in from sixty miles south of the island, having been blown off course by strong northerly winds. Anthony and Sam in their respective boats rowed into Antigua a few days before I made land. Sam then went off to attempt a cycle challenge in America. Anthony did the decent thing, came home, returned to his legal practice, and recently got married. I still keep in touch with him and we meet up for an occasional beer and reminisce about the good old days. There have been so few people who have rowed solo across the oceans that it's good to meet up and relive the highs and lows. It's strange again. We both enjoy our social occasions, but when we say our goodbyes I, and I suspect Anthony, drive home with bittersweet feelings. Of times wistfully and regretfully lost.

Returning home I needed to let my good boatyard friends, Jamie,

Emily and Phil, know of my safe return and, of course, to assure them that their boat designing and building skills had been well proven throughout the voyage. Jokingly they expressed more interest in how the boat fared than me, but I'm sanguine about these things and have recently travelled to Devon again to admire Jamie's new boatyard workshop.

Coming back home was not easy. It hadn't been straightforward when I'd first completed my solo Atlantic sail in 1995, so I was expecting to have to make many readjustments to family and working life. And so it proved. I felt lost and out of sync with people and things around me. Everything seemed to happen in a rush, and I found it difficult to concentrate and accept a return to systems, appointments, schedules and rules. Although I'd needed a routine while at sea I now felt constrained and regimented. I wasn't lost at sea, I was lost at home. Getting back to work was also difficult to accept as a necessary priority, and it took a while to refocus on developing my business and moving it on. Sitting at a desk by a rain-streaked window, it was irksome to pore over the accounts while my inner thoughts still resided in a little craft I'd called home. Everything seemed unreal and I began to question again who I was, what I was doing and why. I had no answers and seemed to be living on split levels. I became a little reclusive about my rowing adventures and was reluctant to talk about them unless pressed – even then I would not be willing to go into much detail. It had happened, I'd enjoyed it, I'd survived. I was back so let's move on.

But an experience like that never truly leaves you and I still find myself in quiet moments glancing back at my logbook, reading my scribbled notes and remembering important and silly little details. I wanted to write this book for the same reasons I wrote *An Ocean Away*, as a legacy for my family, as an inspiration to anyone who dares to defy common sense and follow their own ambition, and as a personal memento for my old age.

Carpe diem. Seize the day. Life is too precious to sit and merely dream.

And, following my own philosophy, that is what I have planned next. I need another challenge and an opportunity to find my own particular freedom again, and yes, it involves the deep waters of the mysterious oceans. Already the sea is tempting me, enticing me back to its unique charms. I need to go.

Why?

Why not?

Dave Clarke, 2012

Appendix

Construction

Boat designer: Phil Morrison
Boat builder: Jamie Fabrizio
Company: Global Boat Works
Electrician: Peter Litton

Departure

La Gomera, Canary Islands
Date: 11th January 2008
Time: 1250 hours GMT

Arrival

Bridgetown, Barbados
Date: 2nd April 2008
Time: 2000 hours GMT
Total miles rowed: 3,235

Total weight loss

3 stones (equal to forty-two pounds), over half a pound per day!
Approximately nineteen kilos.

Metrics

1 nautical mile is equal to 1.15077945 miles. Example, Manchester to London is 181 miles, or if it were measured in nautical miles 157 (181 divided by 1.15).

1 degree of arc of latitude is equal to 60 minutes (1 minute of arc of latitude is equal to 1 nautical mile). To put into context, the earth is a circle of 360 degrees, a degree is 60 minutes (equal to 60 nautical miles as above), then the distance around the world is 21,600 nautical miles (360 times 60) or 24,840 miles (21,600 times 1.15).

Food and water consumption

I had 3 x 5-litre containers onboard and 3 x 1.5-litre drinking bottles. I would use the water maker at least once a day to top up and keep full the 3 x 5-litre containers. These would then be transferred to the drinking bottles as needed.

The water maker would take less than 45 minutes to fill up the 3 x 5 litre containers.

I would rinse off my body most days with a couple of bottles of desalinated water.

Breakfasts

Be-Well packet food. Either muesli or porridge with sultanas. Flapjacks.

Snacks

Everything from chocolate, chocolate raisins, chocolate Brazils, Mars bars, Snickers bars. Various breakfast and cereal bars. Chocolate, plain and raisin flapjacks. Penguins. Breakaways. Peperami sticks. Various packets of biscuits and cakes.

Had some 450 snack bars in total plus the packets, cakes and biscuits etc.

The breaks throughout the day would be snacks and drinks of tea. It was quite usual to have two or three snacks at each break.

Evening meal

Be-Well packet food. Had five flavours for evening meals and two flavours for pudding. I would usually eat two meals and one pudding. Other meals were non-re-hydrating, such as Marks and Spencer's tins of beef steak, mince and chicken. Also specialist packets of fish steaks and long-life meats. Instant mash, rice, pasta or noodles would accompany these meals. Also had various big bars of chocolate and treats for after the evening meal.

Drinks

Apart from a lot of water, tea and coffee were the next popular, and it wouldn't be unusual to have over a dozen mugs in a twenty-four-hour period.

Reading materials

Had the usual pilot books for navigation in the Caribbean.

About twenty-five various reading books, an equal mixture of fact and fiction.

First aid

Tablets. Antibiotics. Painkillers. Anti-inflammatory. Paracetamol.
Suturing needles, stitches. Blister-popping needles.
Various plasters, plaster tape, bandages.
Lots of skin creams, ointments, anti-fungal creams, talc.
Antiseptic wipes, baby wipes.

Pain-relief spray, cream.
Sunblock.
Re-hydrating salts.
Eyewash kit.
Tweezers, sharp scissors, nail clippers.